Raptured

Raptured

A NOVEL ON —
The Second Coming Of The Lord

Ernest W. Angley

WINSTON PRESS
P.O. BOX 1790
AKRON, OHIO 44309

ISBN 0-8007-8172-4

Printed in the United States of America

Raptured

RAPTURED

It was an early spring morning. The frosty air was still crisp with the winter coldness that had not completely taken its departure. The sun was just beginning to peep over the hills with a cheery good morning to old Mother Earth. The smell of spring was in the air, and the birds were singing so loudly it seemed they would surely burst their throats for gladness.

It was just before getting up time for many people in the city of Alabesta when it happened. . . .

Suddenly, hundreds of people disappeared into thin air. If these people had all been in one place, the mystery of their disappearance would not have been so confusing; but they had vanished from every section of the city. The people left behind were appalled at the dreadful catastrophe that had struck their city.

Many people went to sleep Sunday night beside their loved ones and awakened Monday morning to discover that their companion or child had vanished into thin air, taking nothing with them. Almost every home in the city was affected either directly or indirectly. All the babies and small children in the city were gone. Not one was left. In some homes, the husband had vanished and the wife was left; in others, the wife was taken and the husband left.

It was fantastic! People driving cars suddenly vanished, leaving their automobiles to stop as they could. Trains were wrecked without an engineer, and airplanes fell without a pilot.

The inhabitants of the earth were dumbfounded as they awoke and searched in vain for a loved one that was missing. People were running the streets, searching and crying hysterically.

Newsboys intently stood on the street corners with papers hot from the press, shouting excitedly, "Extra! Extra! Read all about it! Thousands of people vanished like magic from the face of the earth about six o'clock this morning! Extra! Extra! Read about the greatest mystery ever to take place in the history of mankind!"

Calls were coming in from other cities, states, and nations. It was the same heart-rending report from everywhere — people had vanished into thin air. There were many and far-fetched ideas regarding the solution of the mystery.

What had happened to the universe that had caused people to disappear suddenly and leave no trace of evidence behind as to what had been their fate? Where were they and what had happened to them was on the lips of thousands.

Only yesterday, Mother Collins had sat in her beloved church and heard the preacher say, "The Rapture!"

Mother Collins sat up straighter in her pew and listened attentively. Her keen eyes were fastened upon the speaker's face so that she would not miss a word.

The message was being proclaimed by a young man about the same age as her son, Jim. As she thought of Jim, a tear rolled down her care-worn face and splattered on her blouse. Surely, he was a bundle of love dropped down from heaven. He had proved such a blessing to her in the trying years after her husband, Jimford, was brought home one night cold in death. She felt, at that time, that life was not worth living; but as she looked down into a little round, anxious face of her boy of three, she realized she did have something to live for. Little Jimmy belonged to her and Jimford. He was their own flesh and blood. That time seemed so long ago as she sat that bright sunny morning and listened to the wonderful message on the coming of her blessed Saviour.

Yes, Fairview was having a revival; and the young preacher, Leo Maspero, spoke with erudite confidence, and his voice rang with the Spirit and power of God.

"In the Old Testament, the Jews were promised by the God of heaven that He would gather them back to the Holy Lands. Since nineteen twenty-one there has been the greatest gathering in the history of the Jews. Today, the Jews are stirred more than they have ever been since God scattered their forefathers among all nations.

"Dear friends, as I read how the Jews are fighting for Palestine, I realize the coming of the Son of God is very near. As we look for the Son of God to make His appearance in midair, and the Church, the Bride of Christ, to be raptured, the Jews are looking for the Redeemer of Israel. They are expecting Him to come to set up an earthly kingdom.

"He made His appearance almost two thousand

years ago; but when Christ was born, they said He was not the Son of God, but an imposter. The prophets of old, Moses, Isaiah, and others, spoke of His coming; so it was not because He came at an unexpected time, but it was because His birth was too humble for them. They could not believe their King would be born in an ox stall and laid in a manger, so they shouted, 'Let Him be crucified, and His blood be on us and on our children!' In ignorance, the Jews crucified their King, the Son of the Most High.

"Today, the Jews are still looking for their Messiah. There is a Man of Sin, or a False Christ, who will possess all the characteristics that the Jews expect of their Messiah, and when he makes his appearance the Jews will accept him as their christ."

As Mother Collins listened, her mind wandered to the late news flashes she has heard and the reports she has read in the newspapers. She felt so languid, and her heart ached within. It is not because she is not ready to go, nor is it because she does not love the Lord and have a desire to be with Him; but her only child, Jimmy, is not ready to meet his Lord.

Oh, if he should be left behind to suffer the tortures of the Tribulation or take the Mark of the Beast . . . . Oh, no! Not that! Not Jim! He must be saved!

The young preacher continued. "In the sixth chapter of Revelation, John said he saw the Lamb open one of the seals and a rider on a white horse go forth with a bow in his hand, and a crown was given unto him, and he went forth conquering and to conquer.

"Some people think this is Christ because the rider is on a white horse, but this cannot be Christ because the Lamb, Christ, is the one to open the seal.

"You may ask, 'Isn't white a symbol of peace?'

"Yes, white is a symbol of peace, and when the Antichrist comes, he will come as a peaceful king. Daniel said by peace he would destroy many.

"When we say 'rapture,' we mean when the Son of God will make His appearance in midair and the Bride of Christ, the Church, will be caught up to be with the Lord.

"Some may wonder or want to know when this Antichrist will come. In the ninth chapter of Daniel, it is recorded that Daniel was praying and wanted to know what was going to happen to his people the Jews. As he fasted, prayed, and confessed their sins, he received this answer from heaven: 'Seventy weeks are determined upon thy people.'

"We understand these to be not ordinary weeks but weeks of years. Sixty-nine weeks of years were fulfilled up to the crucifixion of Christ. The Jewish Dispensation went out and the Gentile Dispensation came in. The Jews have one more week of years or seven years to make out their seventy weeks declared in the Book of Daniel. That time cannot set in until the close of the Gentile Dispensation. The rapture of the Bride will bring to a close the Gentile Dispensation, and then the Jews' seven years will begin.

"You may say that the Church must go through half of the Tribulation; but this cannot be true, according to the Word of God.

"Isaiah 26:20 says, 'Come, my people, enter thou

into thy chambers, and shut thy doors about thee: hide thyself as it were for a little moment, until the indignation be overpast.'

"In the Book of Revelation, one of the seven churches was promised that it would be delivered from the hour of temptation that is to come upon the earth to try all flesh.

"It is not logical for the Gentile Bride to be left here after the Gentile Dispensation has gone out. Also, if we are to go through half of the Tribulation Period, we could wait until the Man of Sin makes his appearance and then count three and one-half years, and we would know when the Son of God will make His appearance and rapture the Church. This is not true. Jesus said no one, not even the angels in heaven, knew the day or the hour of the coming of the Son of God.

"The spirit of the Antichrist is already here, but he cannot be revealed until the Church is gone. I think of the Church as a dam. As the dam holds the water back, the Church keeps the Antichrist out. When the Church is removed, then the Antichrist will rush in and make a covenant with the Jews for seven years.

"In the middle of the week, or the middle of the three and one-half years, the covenant will be broken. At first, the Jews will be completely deceived, and they will think he is the real Christ.

"We do not know what the next news flash will bring. It may mean that Palestine has been opened to the Jews. If this is God's time for the Jews to gather back to Palestine, the Arabians will not be able to keep them out."

As Mother Collins sat there with misty eyes and unshed tears, the birds on the lawn were making melody, and the sun rays played on the stained-glass windows. She felt it was wonderful to be there and hear the message. If only Jim and his wife, Lucille, were saved, it would make the morning complete.

As her mind wandered back to Jim's childhood, she thought of his little, golden-brown head of curls bowed as he earnestly said his prayer. That was always a touching scene to her.

"Now I lay me down to sleep, I pray the Lord my soul to keep. If I should die before I wake, I pray the Lord my soul to take. God bless Mommie, Aunt Jeannie, Uncle Bill, and God bless everybody."

As she had witnessed those beautiful, heart-touching, bed-time scenes, her heart had swelled as she had thought what a wonderful man her Jimmy would be. Who knew, he might be a minister — not that there were any ministers in their family, but God might use him. Many people seem to think things like that must run in the family. Some things might run in families, but when it comes to God's work and God, He calls whomsoever He chooses. That is God's way of doing things. There could be no greater honor bestowed upon Jim than for him to be a minister, chosen and annointed by God to deliver His great spiritual truths.

Once Mother Collins mentioned this to Mrs. Kirkland as they were talking about what they wanted their boys to be when they grew up, and Mrs. Kirkland threw up her hands and cried out in horror.

"A minister!" she ejaculated. "Susie Collins you must be out of your mind to wish such a dull, dreary, irksome life upon your child. Not I! I want my boy to be famous so the world will idolize him. A minister," she drawled. "Oh! Do they ever possess fame? Oh well, you always have been so very old-fashioned and queer. You know what? I love you for it; and if it takes Jim's being a minister to make you happy, I hope he will be for your sake."

As Mother Collins sat reminiscing the conversation, it seemed only yesterday that her son, Jim, was a child. Jim did not choose as his career to be a minister. He was not a child of God, and he was not interested in religion. Law was the most interesting and important concern in his life.

"It looks as if the coming of the Lord is so very near," the minister said. "The signs pointing to His coming have been fulfilled, and He could come anytime and not do an injustice to the Scriptures. Who knows! It might be today!"

Mother Collins had read the Book of Revelation and the Book of Daniel, but the study of the Antichrist was always interesting to her. This young man made it plainer than anyone she had ever heard. He made His coming seem so close that it seemed that every sinner in the building should surrender to the Lord before leaving the service.

The minister was hurriedly going on. "The Antichrist will reveal himself, and the covenant will be made with the Jews. The Jews will rejoice, and, no doubt, the bands will play as the Jews march for joy. Remember, they have been looking a long time for this great event. They will erect their temple in Palestine and offer their sacrifices to God as their forefathers did.

"We might call this man the Little Horn, that Wicked One, the Beast, the Son of Perdition, or other names and still be talking about the same person. The Bible gives him a number of different names.

"I have been told that the Jews have their stones carved and in various ports ready for shipping so they can erect their temple when their Messiah makes his appearance. In just a short time after he makes his appearance, the Jewish people will have their temple erected and ready to offer their sacrifices.

"Daniel tells us, in the Book of Daniel, that craft is made to prosper in his hand. That means that factories and all types of industries will flourish. The Antichrist does something his forefathers did not do; that is, he divides the spoil with the people, and that makes it more convincing that he is the Son of God.

"When Hitler was manifesting such great power, some thought he would be the Antichrist; but Hitler could not have been a Messiah of the Jews because he did not favor the Jews. The Antichrist will favor the Jews above all other people. Hitler had them killed by the hundreds.

"The first three and one-half years will be a peaceful reign, and the Jews will offer their sacrifice to God. One day after the first three and one-half years, the Jews will go up to the temple to worship, and the Antichrist will defile the temple with some unholy sacrifice and set himself up in the temple of God, showing himself that he is God. They do not believe him to be God, but the Son of God, so their eyes will be opened and they will realize that they have been deceived.

"A part of the Jews will flee to the wilderness, where God has a place of refuge prepared for them away from the Antichrist.

"In the thirteenth chapter of Revelation John said, 'And I stood upon the sand of the sea, and saw a beast rise up out of the sea, having seven heads and ten horns, and upon his horns ten crowns, and upon his heads the name of blasphemy.

"'And the beast which I saw was like unto a leopard, and his feet were as the feet of a bear, and his mouth as the mouth of a lion: and the dragon gave him his power, and his seat, and great authority.'"—*Revelation 13: 1, 2.*

"In other words, John said he saw men rise up out of the nations. This is the Antichrist and his governmental power. John goes on to say that all the world wondered after the Beast and they worshiped the Beast. Also, John said they worshiped the dragon, or devil, who gave power unto the Beast.

"In this same chapter, we see another Beast come forth. John said he had two horns like a lamb, he spake as a dragon, and he had power to call down fire from heaven. This is the third member to help make up the Antigodhead.

"In the trinity of the Godhead we have the Father, the Son, and the Holy Ghost; in the Antigodhead, there is the devil, which is the Antigod; the Antichrist, which is the Beast; and the Antispirit, which is the False Prophet.

"As this is a Holy Ghost Dispensation, the Holy Ghost works in the interest of Christ. He is not working to glorify Himself, but the Father and the Son. In that day, the Antispirit will be working to glorify the Antichrist and the devil. He will deceive men with the great miracles he is able to perform and say to them who dwell on the earth to make an image of the Beast.

"'And he had power to give life unto the image of the beast, that the image of the beast should both speak, and cause that as many as would not worship the image of the beast should be killed.

"'And he causeth all, both small and great, rich and poor, free and bond, to receive a mark in their right hand, or in their foreheads.'" — *Revelation 13:15, 16.*

"Let me persuade you to make preparation to meet your Lord. He may appear before another sunrise.

"'Watch therefore, for ye know neither the day nor the hour wherein the Son of man cometh.'"— *Matthew 25:13.*

A hush lingered over the audience, and everything was deathly still. As the minister closed his Bible, the choir began to sing: "Tomorrow May Mean Goodby," and the congregation stood for what, he said, could be the last altar invitation before the rapture.

Conviction gripped the hearts of people in a great way, and some wept aloud. Mother Collins felt the place was covered with God's Spirit. Numbers were going for prayer; but others were standing back, determined not to seek God in that service. They thought they would accept Him sometime in the future, but not this morning.

The last glorious testimony of those who had found Jesus was given, and the audience was dismissed. Amid joy and praise to God for bringing so many into the fold, the people passed slowly out the church door in twos and threes, talking about the wonderful service and how near the coming of the Lord seemed.

Mother Collins walked briskly along the road, with the glory of the Lord shining on her countenance. From a distance, no one would have believed her to be in her sixties, because she walked so spryly. A close view of the kind, old face with the many wrinkles, revealed the metamorphoses from the many years she had trod life's journey.

Hester Bell Wilson sped up from her usual slow pace to overtake Mother Collins. She usually walked slowly, but she wanted to talk with someone this morning.

As she quickened her steps, she wondered why people wanted to spend so much time in church; furthermore, they seem to enjoy it. She just could not understand some people. Why can't people go to the movies and other lively places? It would be a lot more interesting. They said it would not be Christian like, and she did not want people to think she was a little heathen, even though she did not have much religion.

Her cheeks were flushed and her black curls were blowing in the noonday breeze as she hurried to catch up with Mother Collins. With a twinkle in her eyes, Mother Collins looked up into Hester Bell's pretty, round face as Hester overtook her, gasping for breath.

"Hester Bell Wilson, is something after you?" she asked in a merry tone. "Land's sake! A body would think a young girl like you would not be in such a rush to get home on a beautiful day like this."

Hester Bell fell in step with Mother Collins, trying to think of an answer to give her. Hester Bell always had some kind of an answer to give to cover up her real feelings. If she had to tell a lie to be brave, she could do that, too.

"You know good and well I am not rushing to get home. I do declare! Mother Collins, if I didn't know you so well, I would say you saw me trying to overtake you, and you walked a little faster. Anyway, now that I have caught up with you, what do you think of that defiant, insolent message this morning? I have never had so many goose pimples on me in an hour in all of my life. Of all the tommy-rot! That preacher saying the Lord might come just any time. He had me so scared I didn't know whether to run or stay. Although I knew it wasn't true, I was scared within an inch of my life. Couldn't he think of anything more pleasant to talk about? Where did he get all that stuff?"

Mother Collins listened quietly without comment

to such a spasmodic outburst. Suddenly, Hester Bell stopped and looked searchingly down at Mother Collins. Her complacent countenance and quietness confused her more than ever.

"You—you don't believe all he was saying, do you, Mother Collins?"

Mother Collins spoke calmly but convincingly and to the point. "Yes, child, I'm afraid I do. That wasn't something new to me this morning. I have been looking for Jesus for a good many days now."

"You mean it could happen right now as we walk along here together?" inquired Hester Bell.

"That I do, child. I mean exactly that."

Hester felt more goose pimples rise, and a cold chill ran up her spine.

"You mean everybody believes that fantastic story about people being changed in a moment, in the twinkling of an eye, and the dead coming out of the graves?"

"No, I'm afraid everybody doesn't believe it; but I wish all did. It is so sad for anybody to be left behind when our Lord comes."

Hester Bell stared wide-eyed for a moment; then she decided she had better say something that had a little humor in it so she could laugh and get rid of that awful feeling. She thought that the fear she felt was enough to frighten a person out of his wits or shatter his nerves so he would never be any more good. Oh, why did she ever decide to overtake Mother Collins anyway? Never did it cross her mind that anyone would believe such a ridiculous story—not even the minister who told it.

"Well, you can believe such doctrine if you want to; but as for me, I'm too modern to believe anything like that. Nobody could ever sell me on anything so outrageous. I wasn't born just yesterday."

Hester tried to sound convinced and pretend she was not going to let it bother her in the least, but there was a little tremble in her voice that anyone listening could not avoid detecting.

"The very idea," she went on, "of Gretta Helman being caught up in the air. She just weighs about three hundred pounds. Could you ever feature her sailing through the air?"

Hester Bell paused and gave a loud, nervous laugh, but Mother Collins was very sober and composed. Hester Bell felt a big lump come in her throat. What an eerie feeling.

It seemed to Hester a thousand more goose pimples popped out on her.

O tomatoes! she thought. Why does a whole Sabbath have to be spoiled like this? I bet if I live through this I'll never hurry to ask her about anything else.

"Do you realize, Hester Bell, if everybody was expecting the Lord to come this would be a different world?"

Mother Collins' penetrating eyes were sparkling like diamonds as she continued.

"Yes, this would be a different world," she softly said as though she might be talking to someone much closer to her than Hester Bell.

"There would be no movies, no drinking, no card parties, no dancing, no blasphemy, no homes broken up by divorce, no prisons, and no murders or suicides. Yes, indeed, this would be a great world."

Hester, who had been listening attentively, spoke abruptly. "It might be for you, but not for me. Horrors! I hope nobody ever makes me believe a story like that. I would be scared all the time. Why, I would be afraid to go to sleep and afraid not to. I'd be scared to go away from the house and afraid to stay there. Mercy! This gives me the creeps! I have always been afraid of God."

"Dear child, you don't have to be afraid of God. He loves us. In fact, He loved us so much He sent His own Son that we might be born again and have all our sins washed away in His blood. No, child, there is nothing to fear if you are prepared," Mother Collins said.

"What if someone you loved more than anyone else in the world wrote you a letter and said he was coming for you to take you to a beautiful place where there is no sorrow, no heartaches or pain, and you would never be sad again or want for anything? He would tell you that the street in his city was pure, wonderful gold, and the gates were of pearl. You would have a mansion to dwell in, with a river running close by, from which you could drink and live forever. You would not have to fear death. There would be no wicked people. Everybody would love you and you would love everybody. Best of all, your wonderful friend you love so much would live right there in that great city with you. Would you be afraid? Just because this wonderful friend would say he could not tell you just when he would come for you, but for you to be ready to leave anytime, would you be afraid and worry all the time; or would you go about with a song in your heart wishing your dear friend would come that very day?"

"Oh, if I had a friend like that, I would be elated for him to come," Hester answered without hesitating. "Of course, I wouldn't be afraid, but the coming of God's Son is different. I don't know Him," she frankly admitted.

"You have not become acquainted with my dear Lord and taken Him as your personal Saviour," Mother Collins said brightly. "That is the reason you are afraid. If you will only let Him come into your heart, then you need not fear any longer. Jesus is that dear Friend I was talking about. He went away, but He said He would come again and take us to be with Him. You see, child, it is a wonderful thought to know someone loves you and will soon come to take you away from trouble to a place where you will be happy always."

After what seemed an eternity to Hester Bell, they came to the white, picket fence surrounding a six-room white bungalow where Mother Collins lived. At each window hung a neatly starched white, organdy curtain, lazily flapping in and out, scraping the window sill. The red geraniums on the front porch nodded their heads with a cheery welcome. A beautiful, grassy lawn that was kept to perfection and the shrubbery here and there revealed a charming picture.

Hester surveyed the neat, attractive home with dreamy eyes and thought if she lived in a place like that she certainly would not rejoice in somebody coming to take her away.

"I guess here is where I stop. Won't you come in, Hester?"

"Oh, no. I must go home. Mother will be looking for me."

Hester knew her mother never did look for her at a certain time. She just wanted to get away from Mother Collins.

"Better come in and have some fresh cookies with a glass of cold milk. I just baked them yesterday. I thought maybe Jim might bring Baby Sue over. She likes them so much. She always says, 'Mam ma, want kukie! Mam ma, want kukie!' She is such a wonderful child. I wish she could be in Sunday School."

"Come on in Hester," she insisted.

"Oh, no! I'll stop some other time."

Down the street Hester went at a fast pace, licking her lips as she thought about those good, tasty, crunchy cookies. She had to deny herself a spicy treat all because some preacher wanted to scare everybody to death by preaching about God's Son might come just any time and snatch people away. What a world this had turned out to be. Not on your life would she have stopped and eaten cookies, no matter how good they were, and hear more about people disappearing and sailing through the air.

Hester rushed swiftly forward almost afraid to

look up in the sky for fear she might see the Lord. Finally, she arrived in front of a two-story white house, trimmed in yellow. Hester took the stone steps two at a time, rushed across the porch, and burst into the living room.

"Mom, are you home!" she shouted.

Of course, she knew her mother would be there. She was always home that hour of the day. In fact, it would not be long until the gang would arrive to play bridge. Hester did not go in for their wild parties—especially on the Sabbath. Although Hester was not saved, she had a conscience, and it would not allow her to do just anything. She must keep the friendship and good will of people like Mother Collins and her Sunday School teacher. They did not believe in people living and acting just any way.

Hester whisked through the kitchen door, and before her mother could say anything she exclaimed, "Mom, the Lord's coming!"

Susan Wilson looked startled for a moment but answered as quickly as she could gather her wits. "Now who has been putting such nonsense in your head? I declare! You can't send children any place this day and age and feel assured they will not hear something they should not."

"But I should hear this and you and Pop should, too. It isn't a thing that should be kept a secret. The minister said so."

Hester had forgotten that she was supposed to be angry with the minister and should not quote what he said.

"Reverend Maspero said it might be just any time; and according to the Bible, it looks as if it might be right away. If you are not a child of God and walking in the light of God's Word, you will be left behind.

"Mom, the deplorable, horrible things the people that are left will have to go through with. . . ."

Hester began to relate all the message. If the young minister could have heard her, he surely would have had to smile.

When Hester began to tell her mother the story and she saw the fear on her mother's face, she did not fail to mix her imagination with the message. Well, after all, why not let her mom feel a few goose pimples, too? She would not go to church and let the preacher make them rise on her. Hester had felt plenty on her that morning as she listened.

When Hester paused to take a deep breath, her mother blurted out, "Why that's absurd. I don't believe that. People have been telling that for years and years, and it hasn't happened. Nothing but feeble-minded people believe such false doctrine. I was just reading something along that line the other day. A well-educated minister of some big church, I forget what denomination, but anyway, he said some people were forever talking about signs of the coming of Jesus and looking for Him to show up just any time. He said their denomination used to teach that, but they had learned better. He said this is a day of enlightenment, and nothing but the ignorant and uninformed believe such nonsense. Intelligent people don't believe such rot."

"Yes," interrupted Hester, "and he is just like those people in the days of Noah. They refused to believe that water was going to cover the whole earth, and they failed to get ready to escape it. The minister said so," she said with triumph.

Susan Wilson's face turned pale at this, and she stood motionless, in deep thought.

"It's foolish for me to give this any consideration whatsoever," she said with a dry laugh. "Now run along, Hester. We won't speak of this again, and I don't think you need to go back to that church any more. Such stuff as you heard this morning is not good for your nerves."

"Ah, Mom, you must not talk like that about the coming of God's Son. It isn't pleasing to God. Thousands of redeemed saints are looking for Him, and all of those people could not be fooled. Now, could they, Mom?"

Hester looked questioningly at her mother. Hester's mother was too much upset to talk about it any longer, but she would not have admitted it to Hester or anyone.

Hester turned on her heels and mounted the stairs to her room. She changed her blue silk dress to a little red gingham dress with dainty ruffles on the sleeves and waist.

Susan Wilson worked in deep meditation as she prepared luncheon. Yes, she remembered the teachings of her mother who had been planted in the Mother Earth long ago. She, too, had been one of those old saints of God who shouted and rejoiced as she talked about the coming of her Lord. That seemed such a long time ago.

For the last few years, Susan had not thought much about the coming of the Lord. To tell the truth, she could not say for sure how long it had been since she had gone to the Lord's house to hear the message that God intended mankind to hear. What if the Lord would come? The minister said it could be any time. It was such shocking news to know people were honestly looking and believing that Jesus was really coming to catch people away. She was so sure that people of today could not and would not believe a story like that.

About that time Hester bounced into the kitchen, and her mother dropped the carving knife with which she was peeling potatoes and jumped as if she were shot.

"Scare a body to death! I declare! You don't use the wisdom God gave you the day you was born!"

"I'm sorry, Mom," Hester said apologetically. "I didn't mean to frighten you. What's the matter? Are your nerves bad today?"

"Yes! Yes!" she exclaimed nervously as she glanced toward the door as if she might be expecting to see a ghost make his appearance.

At last, lunch was on the table and the three were seated. Hester's father had been out on a Saturday night spree, and, as usual, he did not feel well. He was sullen at the table and did not want to talk, and Hester's mother would jump almost out of the chair at the least noise.

"What has come over this family?" Hester murmured, sliding back her chair. "Nobody seems to want to talk. I think I will go to Nancy's house. Maybe the balloons are all burst there."

Susan looked up with a stern look and austerely said, "You will do nothing of the kind, Hester Bell Wilson."

Her mother always stressed her full name when she was really annoyed with Hester about something. Of course, she blamed Hester with her feeling that the Lord was coming. After all, she was the one who came home and disturbed her peace of mind.

"You will go to the kitchen and wash the dishes. That's where you will go. I am expecting the gang over this afternoon for a game of bridge. Stir the cocoa that is on the stove before you begin. If you will work really fast and do your work thoroughly, you can go to Nancy's," she sternly said. "The gang would rather have the house to themselves, anyway. I hope your Dad will find a place to go, too," she said, giving him a sharp glance.

"But, Mom," Hester replied earnestly, "what if the Lord should come this afternoon while you are playing bridge? Then what?"

Susan looked confused and answered, "Now Hester I mean for you to hush such silly nonsense around here. The Lord is not going to come, and, furthermore, who cares if He does? It is no concern of mine," she said boldly.

What a front of indifference she was putting on, but behind that mask was an uneasy feeling that she could not get rid of.

Hester hurried to finish the dishes, slinging them down hard enough to break, but somehow they managed to remain whole. When she began to wash the pots, it sounded as if she were serenading. What did she care? She felt all people reared children for was to do things they did not want to do.

She began to sing the chorus of, "Our Lord is Coming." The choir had sung it that morning, and it kept ringing in her ears.

Susan Wilson was in her room, dressing for the bridge party. A cold chill ran up and down her spine; and perspiration popped out on her soft skin like rain drops, as she listened to Hester singing.

"For goodness sake, Hester, stop that yelling and go on over to Nancy's. I'll finish the kitchen myself. Maybe I can have a little peace and quietness around here."

That was enough for Hester. No one ever told her more than once to leave the kitchen. She was always ready to go with a smile of triumph.

Hester dashed her face with cold water and gave her black hair a few strokes with the comb which lay on the window sill. Off came the apron, and out the back door Hester ran, to tell Nancy about the coming of the Lord.

Mother Collins was walking up the steps quietly, as Hester hurried down the street past her house.

"My! how I would like to have the energy of that girl," she said aloud, as she watched Hester's swift steps. "I used to have that much," she said with a deep chuckle.

There was no one around to hear Mother Collins say that except her dog, Butch, and he wagged his tail as if to say he believed every word. After she reached down and gave him a big pat on the head and declared that he was the best dog in all the world, she entered the house.

Mother Collins' home was not large, but it was large enough for her. Surely it was a picture-book home if there ever was one. There was a small living room, dining room, kitchen, kitchenette (where Mother Collins ate most of the time), two small bedrooms, and bath. Her Chippendale armchair sat close by the double windows in the living room. An exquisite antique table near the armchair held the precious old Book that Mother Collins loved better than life itself. It had been her greatest comfort in the years gone by. Hour after hour she had searched its deep truths about the God of the universe, and these truths had become endeared to her. The more she learned about Him, the more she loved Him, and the closer she was drawn to Him. Indeed, it was the Book of all books, and it gave her the "blessed hope" she carried in her bosom that Sabbath day.

As she prepared her noonday meal, her mind kept recalling the message she had heard that morning. What a glorious message! True? Yes, it was all true. She had read it again and again in God's Word. Why couldn't everybody see it and get ready?

Jim, her only child, was trained the right way, and he knew about the coming of the Lord. She had prayed so many times for him, but he would not surrender his heart to the Lord. In fact, he had seldom gone to church for the last five years since he married Lucille. Jim was a good moral boy, and she believed that he would make a worker for the Lord if he would give God his life. It might have been different if Jimford had lived, but God always knew best.

The officials of the Universal Bank were given a hint that the bank was going to be robbed one night. Mother Collins pleaded with Jimford not to stay at the bank, but he felt it was his responsibility, as the president of the bank, to help try to avert the calamity and be there if something happened. Something did happen! There was a gun battle between the gangsters, the law, and Jimford. He was shot three times— once through the arm and twice through his heart.

As Mother Collins looked at his cold face, she did not look with eyes of no hope, but she murmured amidst tears, "Jim, I'll meet you." She had the consolation that he was a child of the King, and that was worth more than anything money could buy.

Gnawing pains clutched her heart as she entered the big, empty house that first night after Jim had passed away. With every little noise, she looked for Jimford and wished and hoped that she was dreaming and would wake up and find it all a bad dream. She longed to hear Jimford say, "Mother! Darling! What's wrong sweetheart? You must have been dreaming a dreadful dream."

Jimford left her the big house, they were so proud of, free from debt and a nice, reliable income. The years following Jimford's death were not easy ones.

God had given her a great responsibility (little Jimmy); but the years passed, and her greatest comfort was that the Lord would soon come and take her to her Jimford.

Many men looked upon Mother Collins with admiration, but she did not desire the company of any of them. Her concern for Jim's happiness and welfare was greater than any other interest.

When she dressed Jim for his first day in school, she was so proud of him. If Jimford could see him he would admire his son, but she would not call him back if she could. No! a thousand times no! He was much better off, and she and little Jim would go to him some day.

She always took Jimmy to Sunday School, had a family altar, read the Bible to him each night, instructed him in the ways of God, and brought him up in the fear of the Lord.

When Jim finished high school and left for college, it was hard to see him go, but she could not afford to be selfish because he must be given a chance to be a success in life.

During the third year of Jim's college life, he met the girl of his dreams, Lucille. Mother Collins did not want Jim to go through life without a helpmate, but she feared and trembled because Lucille was not a Christian and had not had the teaching that her Jim had received. From what Mother Collins had been told, Lucille was reared in a home that did not believe in God. Mother Collins tried to talk to Jim and tell him that his marriage would not be successful, but

Jim was young and in love and felt that he could make anything work.

"Jimmy, you need to seek God and let Him direct your steps. He surely has a mate for you somewhere that has been brought up to fear God."

"Oh, Mom, now don't you worry your pretty little head about me. I'm going to live for the Lord some day. You will see. A woman will follow her husband every time. You just wait. Some day you will be glad that I married Lucille."

Mother Collins knew it was no use to say more, so with a heavy heart she tried to smile and bear it with cheerfulness.

Jim and Lucille were married, and Mother Collins tried to act glad and help them to make their married life a happy one. She moved out of the big stone house, that had been her home so many years, to a little white cottage a few blocks down the street. Over the protest of Jim, she gave the old home place to Jim and Lucille for a wedding present. She did not need a big house just for herself.

Things had not worked out as Jim had anticipated concerning the church. He and Lucille seemed to get along splendidly except for that one thing, and, to Mother Collins, that was the most important.

Lucille never had been to Jim's mother's church but twice, and she laughed and made so much fun Jim vowed he would never take her again. Lucille did not believe in the power of God and people shouting. Mother Collins and the saints shouted at her church because they believed in old-time salvation. Jim went to Sunday School awhile without Lucille and sometimes he went to Sunday evening worship alone, but soon he ceased to go.

When Sue came along, Mother Collins got out her sewing basket and began to make dainty clothes for her first grandchild. The baby had brightened up her life a great deal, but still that longing for Jim and Lucille to find the Lord was a great weight upon her heart.

At the age of three, Baby Sue had never been to Sunday School but the few times Mother Collins had taken her. Baby Sue enjoyed it so much and she was thrilled to get the little card with the colored picture on it. Mother Collins recalled the first time Sue's little chubby hand held her first Sunday School card.

The tears rolled down her cheeks as she prayed, "Oh, God, please save Sue's mother and daddy so she can be in Sunday School every Sunday and be taught about You. Your coming seems so near. Help Jim and Lucille to realize You are coming, and make preparations."

When Mother Collins finished her meal, she washed the dishes, swept the crumbs away, and left the kitchen spic-and-span as usual. She went to the living room and sat in her favorite armchair by the double window. The cool breeze chilled her face as it came across the lake that was a short distance away. She could hear the bees buzzing as they worked making honey. How busy, she thought, are we? Are we making honey for the Master? How many people have I talked to about the coming of God's Son? She decided she would go to Lucille and Jim's and tell them about the message that morning. Lucille would not care to hear, but she must tell them and give them warning.

For a few minutes she bowed before the Lord and asked Him to put the right words in her mouth that she should say.

With the glory of the Lord on her countenance and a prayer on her lips, she started for the old stone house that was so familiar to her.

When Mother Collins arrived, Lucille had not started preparing luncheon. They always slept late on Sunday and ate breakfast about eleven o'clock.

"How are my children today?" Mother Collins asked as she entered the house.

"I feel fine, but Lucille has a headache," Jim answered with a yawn. "I suppose she slept too late."

Baby Sue saw her coming and clapped her hands with delight. Mother Collins enveloped her with her strong arms, gave her a big hug, and planted kisses on her rosy cheeks.

"Oh, I wish you two could have been at the morning service and heard the evangelist deliver the most wonderful message I have ever heard on the coming of the Lord."

Lucille's eyes narrowed and her mouth curled up at each end. "Who cares to hear fairy tales? I can read them in a book and sleep late on Sunday morning."

Mother Collins' cheeks flushed and Jim gave Lucille a grave, stern look. Mother Collins had come for a purpose, and she did not intend to be baffled by Lucille's sarcasm.

"It was so wonderful," she went on as if nothing had ever happened. "It looks as if our Lord will soon come for His own."

On and on she narrated the message, not letting up a second to take a deep breath for fear she would be interrupted by Lucille. Lucille could be very unpleasant when she wanted to; and when you talked to her about the coming of the Lord, that was one of the times she tried to be as arrogant as possible.

When Mother Collins finished, Jim sat in silence and his cheeks became very pale. Lucille glared a minute at Mother Collins and then burst forth with a hideous laugh. She laughed until she almost became hysterical.

"Stop it you fool! I said stop!" Jim shouted, but Lucille laughed the harder.

Jim took her by the shoulders and shook her until her teeth chattered, and finally she became silent.

"Of all the rot and unconceivable things I ever heard, that wins the medal. You don't need to think you can come over here and scare me into going to your old-fashioned church, for I am not interested. Do you hear? Once and for all, I am not concerned whatsoever in what goes on over there. If I were going to church, I would not go where a group of fanatics like you go. Not on your life, I wouldn't."

Lucille stood, looked Mother Collins straight in the eye, and with her hard eyes flashing like fire she said, "You let that runt of a so-called preacher make you think you might go sailing through the air almost any time just like that, eh?" she said, snapping her fingers. "Of all the nonsense. I thought you were more intelligent than that. I knew you were a religious fanatic, but I certainly didn't think my husband's own mother would be so foolish as all that."

"Lucille," Jim spoke sternly, "remember that is my mother, and I'll not stand for you to insult her in this way in my own home."

Mother Collins broke in with her sweet, gentle voice that Jim thought no one else possessed but his own dear mother.

"Let her alone, son. I understand. She hasn't had the training in God's truth as you and I have. She just doesn't realize what the Bible has to say about these things. After she unloads and gets all those thoughts out of her system, I think she will feel better."

"Indeed!" blazed Lucille, "not had the training Jim has had! If that is what you call training, I haven't missed a thing. My mother and dad are modern people and too well educated ever to believe such a fantastic tale as that. You couldn't make me believe it if I woke up some morning and everybody was gone but me. People missing! The rapture!" she drawled. "I suppose your disappearance would make front page news," she sneered. "I can see the headlines now."

Mother Collins watched Lucille and listened with a heart full of pity for the girl who had been so unfortunate as to have had a mother and father who did not believe God's Word rear her. If there were only something she could say to break down her unbelief, but she had tried and failed! What else could she do? There was nothing else to do.

"The discussion of God and people being caught away is closed now and forever!" she said with a commanding tone. "I don't want you to ever mention the word 'rapture' to me again. Do you understand? Furthermore, I wish you would stop talking to others about your absurd beliefs. I should dislike for my friends to hear my own mother-in-law talk with such ignorance and childishness. They would never cease to tease me. I couldn't bear that. You are welcome to come to our house any time; but for pity's sake please ditch those notions before you come in. Just don't talk the Bible and God to me at all. I seem to be getting along all right the way I am."

As Lucille rambled on, the tears somehow slipped out and rolled down Mother Collins old, wrinkled cheeks in spite of the desperate effort she put forth to keep them from doing so.

After Lucille calmed down, they sat in silence for a while; then Mother Collins arose to go. Jim and Baby Sue followed her to the door.

"I'm sorry, Mother. Lucille just gets beside herself when someone talks church and God to her."

"I understand, son," Mother Collins answered in a weary tone as if all her strength were about gone.

It seemed to Jim that she had aged years since she arrived a few hours before.

"I'll try never again to mention the subject in her presence. I will just tell my heavenly Father about her when I am on my knees."

"Jim, son," she whispered, "don't let her influence you. Believe me, child, the coming of the Lord is so very near. I know a lot of people are like Lucille. They don't believe it, but the Bible said in the last days there would come scoffers walking after their own lust saying, 'Where is the sign of His coming?' Wouldn't it be sad, Jim, to wake up some morning and find this precious darling of yours gone and then you go over to my house and I'm gone, too? That is what will happen if the rapture takes place, and you haven't been born again. You will surely be left behind."

"Don't, Mother," Jim choked as he placed a gentle hand over hers. "I know you taught me the right way, and I am going to start attending church and give my heart to God. Honest, I am."

"That's fine, son, and then maybe you can win Lucille for the Master."

Mother Collins bent down so Baby Sue could kiss her good-by; then she left.

Jim and Lucille quarreled bitterly after Mother Collins left, and it ended with Jim's sitting in the living room staring at the pages of the newspaper and Lucille in the bedroom, sobbing quietly.

As Mother Collins walked slowly down the street, she thought of her many friends and loved ones that were out of the ark of safety. She must do her best to live a life of influence and win them for the Master.

CHAPTER II

As Hester ran down the back alley toward Nancy's house, she kept repeating over and over again, "He might come today. He might come today." The more she said it, the greater the reality became that Jesus would soon come.

She rushed past Henry Sawyer without so much as a nod, and Henry turned and looked after her in amazement.

"Now, I wonder what's eatin' her? It's not like Hester to act like that," he growled, as he moved doubtfully on up the alley with puzzled thoughts.

Hester had been to Nancy's house so many times it never occurred to her that she should knock. She just opened the door, rushed in, and blurted out, "The Lord's coming!"

"Hester Bell Wilson, what on earth has happened to you, and what are you talking about!" Nancy inquired excitedly.

By this time, Hester had worked herself into a frenzy, and she did not have to put on any to make the occasion seem really important. Saucer-eyed, she delivered her message to Nancy in a dramatical way about the Lord's coming. Nancy was washing dishes, and the plate she held in her hand dropped with a bang and broke into a dozen pieces as she listened to the startling message.

When Hester finished telling the news, tears were blinding Nancy's eyes.

"Why Nancy, what's the matter?" Hester asked.

"I—I'm not—ready—to go," she stammered.

"But you can get ready," Hester replied, amazed at herself for saying such a thing. Then she began to tell Nancy all she could think of about getting ready.

Nancy decided to go that night to the church where Hester went.

When Hester left the house after luncheon, Susan tried to still the fear in her heart. She told herself she had heard that story years ago, and it had not happened yet, so she had nothing to fear. The uneasy feeling kept lingering, and she cried and cried. She tried to convince herself that she was just nervous, and it did not take much to upset her. After she splashed her face with cold water and applied fresh make-up, the door bell rang, and she hurried to let the first guest in to enjoy what she hoped would be a very pleasant afternoon.

When the gang had all arrived and they started playing cards, Susan tried desperately to be gay and lighthearted, to chatter and laugh at nothing; but in spite of all she did, she could not completely hide her emotion.

"Want a cigarette, Susan?" asked Wilma Barnes.

"No, thank you."

"Well, what about a drink? I slipped this from my husband's supply, and it's the real thing. I bet he will pitch a fit when he finds out. Here. Take some."

"No, I don't want any," she said nervously, looking

towards the windows and doors as if someone who did not approve might see her.

"Maybe she's gone religious on us, eh, girls?" Joyce Mason chimed in from across the room.

Susan blushed deeply. She had always been considered a good sport by her gang, and now she was spoiling her reputation all because Hester had gone to church and heard that message on the rapture. Susan felt as if she could spank the very daylights out of her only child for coming home with a message reminding her of what her mother had taught her in her childhood and causing such fear to seize her heart as if judgment was just about to catch up with her. Sunday afternoon was the time for revelry; and here she was, Susan Wilson, the life of a party, acting like a softy. Try as she might, she could not dismiss that statement Hester made—"Mom, the Lord's coming." It kept hammering over and over in her brain, until she felt she would surely go insane.

Wilma leaned forward, gave Susan a scrutinizing look and said, "Susan Wilson, you are actually pale. You look as if you might fall over any moment. Maybe a drink of water would help you."

As she started for the water, Susan lifted her hand in protest and motioned for her to be seated.

"I don't need any water! There is nothing wrong with me, and for pity's sake will you please leave me alone? Just because I don't want a cigarette or a drink, is that a sign that I must be about dead? Now once and for all, please leave me alone! Do you understand?"

Her voice was lifted to a high, nervous pitch by this time, and Wilma's cheeks flushed crimson.

"Well, you don't need to be so nasty about it," she answered sarcastically. "I just wanted to be kind, but some people don't appreciate kindness nowadays."

"Girls! girls!" Mildred Wineheart interrupted, "Let's don't ruin the afternoon because you two are at each other's throats all the time. Come on, Susan, and take a hand in this game. It will refresh you."

"No, I don't want to play another game. If you girls must know, there is something wrong with me. I am sorry, Wilma, if I offended you. I know you girls will laugh when I tell you what it is and say it is all a lot of nonsense. I have tried to tell myself that it is my nerves, but I can't get rid of it."

The gang was all ears. If anyone liked a bit of gossip better than they, one would not know where to start to find him.

"Go on, Susan," Mildred encouraged when she hesitated. "Tell us all about it. You know we are your best friends, and you can confide in us."

"Yes," chimed in Wilma who was, by this time, feeling better toward Susan.

"Well, it was like this. I was feeling just fine this morning until Hester came home from church."

"So it's Hester," interrupted Willie Mae Lamb. "I declare, children this day and time are nothing but trouble."

"Oh, it isn't anything Hester has done; that is, not exactly." She remembered she did hold Hester responsible for part of it, because she did not ask her to come in and tell her about the message on the coming of the Lord.

"Hester rushed in while I was preparing luncheon, and the first thing she said was, 'Mom, the Lord's coming!' It made me so weak you could have knocked me over with a feather. Of course, I told her to hush such nonsense; but she was so full of that message she heard this morning on the coming of the Lord at church until I couldn't stop her. She just had to tell me all about it. I wish she were here and could tell you as she told me, but I would hate to have to listen to her excited voice telling it again and making it seem so real until you can almost imagine it is going to happen just any moment. I'll tell you all that I can remember."

While the gang sat there with their mouths open, alert ears and their eyes like saucers, Susan told the simple message of the coming of the Son of God. As she approached the close, she paused a moment and looked from one to the other. To some this was entirely a new story, and it sounded like a new fairy tale. To others, it stirred old memories of their training during childhood days to respect and believe God's Word. Great fear captured their hearts, and they began to breathe faster and their hearts pounded madly within.

"As you have noticed in the papers, the Jews are

trying to take over the Holy Land. God has promised them in His Word that He will some day gather them back."

When Susan finished, they sat dumbfounded, staring at one another. A minute seemed a long eternity as the swinging of the pendulum of the clock on the mantel shouted, "The Lord's coming! The Lord's coming! The Lord's coming! The Lord's coming!"

"Now, tell me I'm crazy," Susan exclaimed, "but I can't get it off my mind! I'm scared to be alone, and it seems I'm expecting some one all the time."

About that time, footsteps fell on the front porch. Every face became bloodless, and a deep hush came over the crowd. All was quiet, and they sat expecting—they did not know what. It was like a tomb.

Then, the knob of the front door turned slowly, and the door was thrown open. Everyone jumped and gave a shriek; then settled back in her chair, embarrassed and confused as Frank Wilson came into the room.

"What's going on around here? You women act as if I might have been someone who had come back from the dead."

"Why, there's nothing wrong with us," Susan answered, trying to hide her emotion. "It startled us when you opened the door so quickly, and we were not expecting anyone. Why don't you learn to come in more quietly?"

Frank ascended the stairs and passed out of sight.

"Now, Susan, I have been thinking about what you

have just told us, and I don't believe a word of it.
It isn't because it's true that it bears on your mind,
but your nerves are probably bad. Sometimes when
I listen to a murder story over the radio, I feel as if
somebody is going to grab me from every nook and
corner, but the feeling gradually wears off. This is
the same thing. It's just a horrible story somebody
made up, and it is working on your nerves. I wouldn't
give it another thought," Wilma said, making a gesture with her hand and shrugging her shoulders as
if it were all settled.

The party broke up with some trying to be gay;
but somehow the spirit of gaiety had flown, and no
one was able to recapture it.

When the last one had gone, Susan looked all around
her, tiptoed over to the foot of the stairs and listened.
She could hear Frank breathing deeply, and she knew
he was sleeping soundly. With a sigh of relief, she
moved slowly toward the desk and pulled out an old
worn Bible with yellow pages from the bottom drawer.
It had been a long time since she had read her mother's
precious Bible. Every part of Scripture on the coming of the Lord was marked, and Susan turned from
one chapter to another, reading every one of them.
Her heart became heavier and heavier. Indeed, the
Spirit of the Almighty was dealing with her heart. As
she turned to the Book of Revelation and began to
read, a greater fear possessed her. The dreadful things
she read that would happen after the Church, the

Bride of Christ, was taken, was something dreadful to think about, much less experience.

"It isn't a fairy tale," Susan spoke aloud. "I don't care what Wilma has to say about it. I am sure it is God's own Word."

For a long time Susan sat misty-eyed, staring down into the pages of Revelation, thinking. She knew she should be living for Him, and by all means, she should have brought Hester Bell up to fear the Lord as her mother had trained her. Hester had never heard her pray and had not known what a home was like with a family altar. Susan resolved she would start going to church in the near future.

At six-thirty, Hester came in, her face still flushed with excitement. She had told more than one about the wonderful message she had heard at Fairview church that morning. Fairview was not a popular church with some of the town people, and they thought she was too quaint in her ways and preaching that people had to be saved through the blood.

"The very idea," Pat Loveman scoffed, "of this modern day preaching—a bloody slaughterpen religion."

Some of the other churches in Alabesta used to preach about the blood and sing about the blood of the Son of God, but they did not any longer. They thought they had learned better and were too up-to-date to believe a story so outmoded.

Fairview church was persecuted by many, but God had blessed and prospered it. Although people called the members "a group of fanatics," they still held to the fundamental teachings of the Word of God, and most of the members lived pure, clean lives. There were some who claimed to live right who did things they should not, but that was to be expected. In every church, one usually finds some who do not live right; but the fact that there are a few hypocrites in the church will not excuse others for not living for God and serving Him in the beauty of Holiness.

Hester was not ashamed of the church she attended, and nobody better not say anything against the Fairview church in her presence, or she would give them a piece of her mind. Hester was not a member of Fairview, but she intended to be some day.

"Are you going with me to church this evening and hear that wonderful preacher, Mom?" asked Hester Bell.

Susan fixed her mouth to say, "I believe I will," but something within her was fighting with all the voices of darkness saying they would not go tonight. Some other time would do, and there was plenty of time for her to start going to church. She had a slight headache, and that was enough excuse.

"I don't believe I will go this time," she answered quickly, "but you can go and tell me all about it when you come home."

"But, I thought you did not want me to tell you about it at lunch today."

"Well, maybe I didn't, but can't I change and enjoy listening to such tales?"

At last, Hester was ready; and as she glanced down at her watch, wondering if Nancy were really going with her, she heard Nancy coming in the door.

"I'm here, Hester Bell. Are you ready?"

"Sure. We'd better hurry, or we won't get a seat."

Hand in hand, they swiftly walked toward Fairview church. Susan stood at the window and watched them go, wishing she dared go, too.

The church was almost full when Hester and Nancy arrived. Nancy was surprised to see so many people at a church, because the church she attended dismissed services on Sunday evenings so the members and the pastor could go to the movies and other places of amusement.

"They always have a large crowd here on Sunday," Hester remarked. "We'd better get a good seat because they will all be taken soon. Many always have to stand on Sunday evenings."

Nancy looked the congregation over and wished Fairview were her church. The people with their peculiarities were so interesting.

Before the first song began, every seat was taken, and chairs were brought out from the Sunday School Department.

When the first song began, Nancy realized more than ever that this church was drastically different from the one she attended. Never in all her life had she heard such wonderful, melodious singing. It sounded like a heavenly chorus. The singers looked so holy.

Their faces were lighted with the glory of God, which gave them a saintly appearance; but Nancy did not call it the glory of God because she did not know too much about God's glory. As the choir burst forth with "This is Like Heaven to Me," Nancy took a long, deep breath. For the first time, she learned the real meaning of that song.

After the singing, praying, and testimonies were over, Leo Maspero stood in the pulpit and announced his subject—"Great Tribulation." Hester Bell and Nancy sat in a state of terror, as the minister proclaimed, from the Book of Revelation, the horrible things people would have to go through who missed the rapture. Nancy could hardly believe what she heard because she had never known such things were in the Bible. Her pastor never preached a message like that, and he did not talk about the rapture.

A cold, icy hand enveloped her heart as she wondered if her pastor was really saved. She wondered if he had a "born-again" experience like Hester had told her about that afternoon. He never invited people down to the altar to pray as Hester said they did here. He always said if anyone desired to take fellowship with the church, he may come forward and take a front seat; but Hester said that would not save anybody. If The Reverend Maspero had not read passages of Scripture from the Bible, Nancy would not have believed all he said was in the Bible—it seemed so fantastic.

At last, the message came to an end, and the altar invitation was given. Scores of people, it seemed to Nancy, were almost running for the altar. Great fear gripped the entire congregation. People were crying as they rushed toward the altar. Nancy began to tremble, and two, big tears blurred her vision as she thought the Lord was coming and she was not ready.

A small, still voice whispered to her to go to the altar. She gave Hester Bell a furtive glance. Hester was standing like a statue of marble, but little did Nancy realize the great battle that was going on inside her bosom.

"Let's go down there," Nancy choked, hardly above a whisper.

Hester continued to stare into space with unseeing eyes. She heard what Nancy said; but she was fighting hard to keep from going to the altar, so she acted as if she did not hear her. She was not ready to change her way of living tonight, but she intended to go to the altar sometime.

Nancy waited as long as she could, until it seemed that if she did not go, she would die. With all the strength she could gather, she broke away from the clutches of the devil, ran down the aisle to the altar, lifted her hands and head toward heaven, and poured her heart out to God.

Hester Bell looked after her and tried to make a move in her direction, but she just could not—not tonight.

The saints gathered in the altar, and someone knelt

beside Nancy and gave her instructions how to be saved. With tears streaming down her cheeks, Nancy cried out to the God of heaven for Christ's sake to wash away her sins, until she felt the burden of sin roll away. Never had she felt so happy and free at heart in all her life as she shouted the praises of God for saving her soul.

Hester and Nancy walked home almost in silence. Hester Bell was thinking she should have given God her heart, and Nancy was happy because she had just entered God's great sanctuary a short while ago. It was all so strange and new to her. She felt so sacred and holy it did not matter if no one spoke to her. In fact, just now, she did not care to talk to anyone.

Later, they arrived at the gate in front of Hester's house and parted—one with a light heart, and the other with a heart like lead.

Hester stood and watched Nancy as she skipped down the street—neither realized what tomorrow would bring. Hester never once thought that she would live this night over in her mind a thousand times before she died.

As Hester strolled up the steps and on into the house, the face of Mary Conway haunted her. Mary attended Fairview church long before Hester ever knew there was such a place. No one could exceed Mary in living a good, moral life, but she was not a Christian. Her mother and father were both wonderful saints of God. Hester thought if she had a good

Christian mother and father like Mary, she would surely live for the Lord.

Mary had stood back, as Hester had done that night, thinking that some day she would seek the Lord, but not tonight.

At last, Hester went to bed, her last thought being that she must make preparation for the Lord's coming. As she slept and dreamed of green pastures and beautiful trees and flowers, something horrible and shocking happened!

CHAPTER III

Lucille was sick during the night, and Baby Sue was so restless she cried frequently during the night. Jim was up almost all night. Lucille suffered intense pain at times, and Jim tried various home remedies to try to relieve her suffering. Occasionally, he went to the nursery to see about Baby Sue.

The night seemed endless, but at last the dawn came. About six o'clock, Baby Sue stopped her crying. Jim was so busy trying to help Lucille find some ease, he did not go to see about Baby Sue after her fretful cry had subsided.

Lucille's pain became more severe as the hours passed. Jim would have gone for his mother during the early part of the night, but he hated to awake her; and, too, that very day Lucille had talked so disrespectfully to her. Of course, his mother would have come, because he was sure she held nothing in her heart against Lucille; nevertheless, he would not go for her until Lucille asked him to. She always wanted his mother when she became very ill, and he felt she would call for her soon. She had told Jim, more than once, his mother knew just what to do to help someone in pain.

At last, Lucille was saying just what Jim had been listening for.

"What time is it, Jim?"

"Almost seven o'clock," he answered as he came closer to the bed.

"I wish you would go get your mother. I am suffering intense pain," she said in a low voice.

"All right, sweetheart, I will go."

As he went for his hat, Lucille called after him, "Hurry, Jim, I am so sick. Maybe she will know something that will give me relief."

Jim passed by the closed nursery door without stopping to look at Baby Sue. He would have gone in to see about her, but Lucille was in such pain and wanted him to hurry.

If Jim's mind had not been so preoccupied, he would have listened to the excited voice of the newsboy on the opposite corner, but he passed without giving him so much as a glance.

Mother would be up by this time, and the house would be spic-and-span and everything in its place. Mother would be at the double window in the old armchair reading the Bible—the Book that had been so familiar to him in his childhood. Yes, mother would have already prayed her early morning prayer. He was so glad he had a mother who knew how to pray. He could see her, in his imagination, with her silvery head bent over the Holy Book.

As he came in sight of the house, he did not see her at the window where she usually sat at this hour. He hoped his mother was not sick, too, especially with Lucille so sick.

As his foot touched the porch he began to call, "Mother!"

It was not unusual for Jim to call his mother before

he got inside the house. That was one of his old boyhood habits. Lucille had scolded him often and told him it was not good manners, but Jim continued to do as he had always done since he could remember.

This morning, there was excitement in his voice as he threw open the front door and called, "Mother! Mother!"

All was quiet. If Jim had not been in such a hurry and so concerned about whether his mother was sick, too, he would have noticed a peculiar atmosphere in the room.

On into the dining room and kitchen he went, calling, "Mother, where are you?"

As he strained his eyes looking out the kitchen door trying to see if he could see her in the garden, it came to him like a flash that if she were sick, the bedroom was where she would be. Why hadn't he thought of that sooner?

He made a dash for the bedroom where his mother slept. He stood in the middle of her bedroom as one glued to the spot at what he saw. Mother was not there! It looked as if someone had begun making the bed and had put on the sheets, and the quilt was dropped about halfway on the bed.

Jim's wild eyes searched the room but without consolation. Then, it seemed as if someone stuck a dagger in his heart as he thought of the words his mother spoke yesterday—"go over to my house and find me gone."

"Oh, no!" he exclaimed with a choking noise.

"Please, God! Not that! I couldn't bear it!"

Then he shrugged his shoulders, and with a sheepish grin he said aloud, "My nerves must be about shot from staying up all night."

"The rapture has taken place! The rapture has taken place!" kept hammering in his brain, until Jim thought if it did not stop he would lose his mind.

Suddenly, for the first time, Jim noticed the queer atmosphere in the room; and as he looked down on the floor beside the bed, he saw his mother's clothes and glasses lying on the floor. One cold chill after another played up and down his spine.

"No! No! It can't be," he choked. "I won't believe it! My mother can't be gone! Please, God," he begged, "if the rapture hasn't taken place, I'll get right with You. I make a vow," he said with tears blinding his view of the room, "if the rapture hasn't taken place, I will go to the next service and surrender my life to You."

Something, as a great magnet, drew Jim to the living room. On the table lay mother's black Bible. It was open, and as Jim stared at the page, the underlined scripture: "Therefore be ye also ready: for in such an hour as ye think not the Son of man cometh," (*Matthew 24:44*), leaped to his eyes.

Beads of cold sweat popped out on his forehead, and he cried, "It's happened! It's happened! My God! the rapture has taken place, and I have been left behind! My mother is gone!"

With tears flowing down his cheeks, he fell limply

to the floor and wept bitterly before the Lord. How long Jim cried and prayed, he never knew.

Butch, Mother Collins' dog, scratching and whimpering at the front door, brought Jim to his feet.

Slowly, he opened the door, fell on his knees, threw his arms around Butch's neck and screamed, "She's gone, Butch! She's gone!"

Butch sadly nestled a cold nose to Jim's face as if he understood. Suddenly, Jim thought of something which brought him to his feet with a jerk. He dashed down the walk and out the front gate like a madman.

"No! No!" he kept saying. "I pray God you haven't taken my baby. It's enough that my mother is gone, but you can't have Sue. She is mine! I tell you, she is mine!"

His feet just would not move fast enough. Was he dreaming? He had dreamed of trying to run and his feet would not move fast. Could this be one of those dreadful dreams?

When he had gone two blocks down the street, he heard the excited voice of the newsboy saying, "Extra! Extra! Thousands of people disappeared this morning about six o'clock! It seems as if the earth just opened and swallowed them! Read all about it! Extra! Extra!"

Jim rushed madly on, not taking time to get a paper. What did it matter about the details? The main concern now was his baby.

The newsboy said about six o'clock the rapture took place, and he had not heard Baby Sue cry since then. A great storm of thoughts entered his mind as he ran a little faster. The wind blew his hair in his eyes, causing them to sting dreadfully, but what did it matter about burning eyes and tousled hair at a time like this?

He burst into the front door as if a great legion of devils were in pursuit. Not giving Lucille a thought, he ran to the nursery door and threw it open. The nursery bed was empty! He stood there speechless and glued to the spot. He tried to move his lips, but words would not come. He tried to move toward the bed, but he did not have the strength.

Lucille called frantically from the bedroom, but for the moment it did not seem to matter. Mother was gone and now his precious baby had disappeared. He would give anything in all the world to wake up and find that he had been dreaming, but it was not a dream. The rapture had really taken place. Never again would he tiptoe to the nursery door and peep in at a mass of golden curls lying on a soft white pillow.

"My God!" he murmured. "Why didn't I make preparation to meet You? What a fool I have been."

Lucille kept calling, "Jim! Jim! Is that you?"

Lucille wondered who could have rushed into their house like that? The noise sounded awful. Surely, Jim would not come into the house in such a rage—especially when she was sick—unless something terrible had happened. What could have happened, or was it someone else? Could her child be in danger?

The thought of her child being in danger renewed

her strength. Although in great pain and weak from suffering, she managed to slide out of bed. Step by step she crept, making as little noise as possible, as she did not know who might be in the house. Each step she made sent hot pains like fire through her body. After what seemed hours, she reached the nursery door. A man standing in the room with his back to the door startled her; then she recognized him to be her Jim.

"Jim!" she cried with a shrill voice.

Every nerve in her body was on edge, but it was such a relief to find Jim in the nursery.

Hearing his name called brought him back to consciousness of his surroundings, and whirling around he said, "Oh!"

When Lucille saw Jim's pale, drawn face and his glassy eyes, she knew something horrible had happened. Yes, she knew, but what was it?

"What is wrong, Jim?" Lucille demanded.

"They are gone! They are gone!" he exclaimed, and the tears began to flow again.

He had not intended to tell her about the baby until she was well, but two shocks so close together were more than he was able to master.

He stood there and cried and cried as if he had no power to stop. He could not say another word for some time.

"Who's gone, Jim? Tell me! Get control of yourself. I have never seen you so beside yourself!"

Raptured

"Our baby, Lucille, is gone! Can't you under-stand? Our own precious darling is gone!"

Lucille was so weak she had sat down on a stool at the side of the door, but when the statement was made that her child was gone, the shock brought her to her feet.

"Gone!" she cried wildly. "Where is she, Jim? Oh, Jim, get the police. Our baby has been kidnaped! I told you I was afraid for her to sleep in here by herself, but you said it wasn't good for a child to sleep in the room with grown-ups. Now, you see what has happened," she wailed.

Jim stood there without saying a word. Nothing seemed to matter—not even an outburst from Lucille.

"Jim, call the police!" she cried again, but Jim did not move.

Lucille dashed to the telephone just outside the nursery door and dialed police headquarters.

"Lucille," Jim called, "there is no need to call the police!"

"What do you mean?" she asked, placing the re-ceiver back on the hook.

"Lucille, the rapture has taken place," Jim stated with a calm voice, but his brain was going in wild circles.

This world had stopped turning as far as Jim was concerned.

"What do you mean?" Lucille cried with great fear closing in on her.

"Lucille, do you not understand? The Lord has

come! Mother is gone! Our baby is gone! Thousands of others have disappeared, and you and I have been left behind," he choked. "You remember, Lucille, you told mother yesterday never to mention the word rapture to you again. Well, she won't ever trouble you again!"

The word rapture loosed his tears, but he went on. "Maybe you will be satisfied now! She's gone! She is caught away to be forever with the Lord, and Baby Sue is with her. Do you understand?" he sternly said. "You said you did not believe it and made light of the idea, but it has happened, and they are gone!"

Things began to get dark before Lucille, and her head began to whirl around and around. She tried to sit down, but she fainted and fell at Jim's feet. Jim stared down at the crumpled heap, but he did not offer to go for water. His brain was so numb from shock that he could not think what he should do.

The woman from the house behind them began to scream, "My children are gone! Help! Help! Something dreadful has happened to my children! Please, somebody help me!"

Jim was too absorbed in his own trouble to be of any help to anybody.

"Oh, if only I had made the rapture!" Jim muttered. "I had so many opportunities to get right with God, but I put them all off, thinking I had plenty of time."

As he stood over Lucille thinking of his past, he thought of the many times his mother had given him warning. Only yesterday she had warned him. He always put her off until a future date, and now the rapture had taken place. He never thought it would come in his day. People had talked about it for generations, but it had not happened until today, and he and Lucille were not ready.

Lucille moaned softly as she regained consciousness. At last, Jim went to the bathroom and came back with a glass of water and a wet towel. He lifted her head off the floor, bathed her face with the cool towel, and pressed the glass to her parched lips; then he picked her up and took her back to the bed as if she had been a mere child. He tried to console her as she came back to realization of what had happened.

"I want my baby! Please, Jim, find my baby," she kept crying.

Jim tried to tell her they could get ready and go to mother and Baby Sue, but Lucille seemed not to hear.

Jim called the doctor's office, but no one answered; then he remembered it was not his office hours, so he dialed the doctor's home. No one answered. What an awful uproar the world must be in, Jim thought.

He decided he would go to the drugstore and get some sleeping tablets. It would not do for Lucille to go on and on in a rage like this.

Jim felt he would welcome death. What had he to live for with his mother and baby gone? But, life must go on, although sorrow and heartache comes one's way and it seems one cannot live.

The morning edition of the Alabesta *Tribune* lay on the porch, and beside it was another paper printed in red and black. Jim picked it up; and when he unrolled it, the big, black and red boldface type words —THOUSANDS OF PEOPLE MYSTERIOUSLY DISAPPEARED—danced before his eyes.

Wide-eyed and breathlessly he read an account of what had happened. One man said he and his wife awoke about five o'clock and everything was as usual. He heard his wife praying about five-thirty, as she was accustomed to doing, and around six o'clock she put breakfast on the table. He was sitting at the table waiting for her to pour the coffee, and suddenly, a queer feeling came over him. He glanced down at his watch; and as he did, he felt a sweeping wind. When he looked up, the chair was empty and his wife was gone. He could scarcely believe his eyes. She was there just a moment before. He rubbed his eyes and looked again, but his wife was still gone. She could not have gotten out that quickly without his seeing her. He sat there puzzled, trying to figure it all out. She had disappeared as if by some kind of magic. He called her name and searched the house inside and out, but he could not find her. As he thought maybe she was trying to play a joke on him, he went back to the table and tried to eat, but the feeling of uneasiness still lingered.

The radio in the kitchen was playing soft music; and like a bolt of lightning, the program was interrupted, and the most excited voice he had ever heard over a program of that kind began to speak.

"This program is being interrupted for a late news bulletin of great importance. About fifteen minutes ago, the most unusual happening that has ever occurred in the history of our nation took place. Hundreds of people mysteriously disappeared. We have no further information as to detail. Stay tuned to this station for latest developments."

He said it came over him like a flash what had happened. The Son of God had come and taken His Bride, the children of God.

There were more and many other similar experiences, but Jim had to hurry to the drugstore.

Jim was surprised to see the sun still shining and the birds singing. There was nothing to be happy about. Why shouldn't the whole world be black and weeping with great sorrow?

Just then, the front door of Alma Wilcox's house across the street opened and there stood Alma. Jim blinked his eyes with astonishment and stared in unbelief.

"Jim!" she screamed hysterically, "come here at once. My daughter's twin boys are missing. I can't find them anywhere. They stayed with me last night, and around five o'clock when I was up to look about them, they were sleeping peacefully, but now they are gone! I have searched the house over, and I can't find a sign of them anywhere. The doors were bolted from the inside as I had left them last night, and they are too small to have climbed out the window. Their clothes are still in the bedroom. I just tried to get the police, but the line is busy. Won't you please come to help me?"

Jim stood still as a statue. Not a muscle twitched. After he got over the first moment of surprise of knowing that Alma Wilcox had been left behind, her life began to pass through his mind as she rushed madly on with her story. Funny how one's mind will work under severe circumstances.

Alma Wilcox belonged to the same church Jim's mother belonged to, but she never was the devout Christian that his mother was. When the evangelist came to town for a revival campaign, she never had time to attend. When the ladies of the church met for prayer, she always had other plans. Midweek prayer service was the same way. When she did go to church, she never showed much zeal for the lost. While the saints of God pointed the way of salvation to the lost, she usually sat and looked on. Now, the rapture had taken place and Alma Wilcox, in a lukewarm condition, had been left behind.

"My God! woman, don't you know what has happened? The Lord has come!"

Alma's hands and arms began to shake, and her knees began to knock together.

"No! it can't be true!" she cried. "Stop trying to fool me. I am still here. Wouldn't I be gone, too?"

As Jim saw the fear mingled with unbelief, he held up the paper that he had been reading so she could read the boldface type words which covered three-fourths of the page — "THOUSANDS OF PEOPLE MYSTERIOUSLY DISAPPEARED."

From her lips came the most pitiful wail Jim had ever heard come from the lips of a human being.

"My Lord! It's true! He has come and I have been left behind!"

She fell upon her knees in the yard and cried and prayed as she had never prayed before.

"Oh, God, how foolish I have been. Halfheartedly I served you. Like Peter of old, I followed afar off. Why, oh why, did I let the devil deceive me so? Now it's happened! I'm left! I'm left!" she screamed.

Then, an idea struck her. Maybe it was not true after all. If she could find people she knew to be true saints of God were not gone, then she would know.

Arising to her feet in great haste, she rushed for the back gate and down the back alley to a little cabin where old Lily, the scrub woman, lived. Alma felt in her heart if there ever was a true saint of God, surely Lily was one. The old cabin, neat as a pin but unpainted, looked lonely and deserted this morning.

Alma's heart pounded with fear as she approached the closed door. She rapped loudly and waited anxiously. Everything was still. She could hear the loud tick, tick of the clock on the dresser inside, and it seemed to be saying, "You've been left behind! You've been left behind!" Oh, if only Lily would open the door and say, "Howdy, Mrs. Wilcox," in her deep Scottish voice, but there was no answer. She almost imagined she heard a noise on the inside, but the door did not open. Lily was gone! Tears blinded her vision as she stumbled down the steps and back up the alley again.

As she came around the side of her house, she saw Jim standing just where she had left him, staring into space. He looked as if he had aged fifteen years since yesterday. His shoulders, which had always been held straight, were stooped now in despair. His hair was tousled and he had such a haggard look.

As she approached him, she tried to sound calm as she called him and said, "Jim, I just went over to Lily's cabin, and she must have stepped out somewhere. She was not there."

With this, she burst into tears. Jim just kept staring into space as if he had not heard.

At last, Jim awoke from his daze and took notice of his surroundings. He heard a loud knocking on someone's door down the street, and looking straight ahead, he saw Alma standing at the open door of Zelma Prick's. Jim knew the story of the rapture and people being gone was being told to someone else. A scream pierced the air. Another soul had realized Jesus had come, and she had been left behind!

Jim's brain was numb and he felt cold all over. Beads of icy sweat covered his forehead.

As he came near Zelma Prick's gate, Alma and Zelma dashed out the gate and down the sidewalk in front of him. They were clinging to each other as if both felt the other meant life to her. Both their faces were pale and their eyes were pools of torture.

Jim passed by houses with blinds still drawn, and he wondered if anyone had gone from them. What sadness there will be for those who still sleep, he thought, when they awake and become aware of what has taken place.

Jim was so deep in thought that he did not notice the figure of a woman hurrying up the street toward him, and before he realized it, he had bumped into her. It was so unexpected it almost startled him out of his wits. He looked down into eyes that looked as if they had been through a hell of torture, and the great agony was still stamped upon the soul.

"Have you seen my husband and baby? I can't find them anywhere," she wept. "I awoke this morning and they were both gone. My David was such a good boy. I know some dreadful thing has happened to him."

Jim looked at her with eyes of pity. He knew what she must be suffering. Must he tell her the truth? He tried to move his lips and speak the word rapture, but it would not come. He unfolded the paper he was carrying with a vice grip, and without a word, he held the bold, black and red type headlines before her eyes. She stared at it and read it over a couple of times before it seemed to penetrate her mind; then suddenly, she gave a loud shriek and fell to the sidewalk.

Jim rushed on blindly, trying to fight back the tears. He had heard people try to tell what it would

be like just after the rapture took place, but no one
had ever been able to give an example of it.

Jim saw Alma and Zelma hurrying up the steps of
The Reverend Hilary's home—the pastor of Mother
Collins' church. Both pounded frantically on the door.
He waited hoping against hope that the door would
open and the dear old saint of God would not be gone.
He knew if he were home, the rapture would not have
taken place. After waiting at the gate for what seemed
an eternity, Jim passed on down the street. He knew
there was no use in waiting any longer because there
was no one at home.

At last, Jim came to the drugstore. No one was in
the drugstore except the druggist, Bill, who slept in
the back. Jim was his first customer. His grave face
brightened as Jim walked in.

"Morning Jim," he said with a cheerful ring. "How
are you feeling this morning?"

"Terrible," Jim managed to answer.

What was wrong with Bill? How could anyone
ask how a person was feeling on a morning like this?

Bill noticed Jim's pale face and his haunted eyes
and asked, "Jim Collins, what on earth has happened
to you? You look as if you are about ready to col-
lapse."

"My baby and mother have disappeared," Jim replied.

Bill stared goggle-eyed and asked, "Your what!"

Jim held up the newspaper he was still carrying;
and as Bill read the bold headlines, the bottle of medi-

cine fell from his hands and crashed on the floor.

"You—you—don't mean your baby—and mother —were in that number?"

"Yes, that is exactly what I mean. Lucille is in a terrible condition, and I want some sleeping tablets to get her quieted."

With trembling hands Bill managed somehow to lift the sleeping tablets from the shelf.

He, too, had been reared in a home where there was a family altar and a silver-haired mother who read God's Word and possessed the "blessed hope." She had died years ago, but he remembered one of her favorite scriptures from Paul's writing, which was:

"Behold, I shew you a mystery; We shall not all sleep, but we shall all be changed,

"In a moment, in the twinkling of an eye, at the last trump: for the trumpet shall sound, and the dead shall be raised incorruptible, and we shall be changed.

"For this corruptible must put on incorruption, and this mortal must put on immortality.

"So when this corruptible shall have put on incorruption, and this mortal shall have put on immortality, then shall be brought to pass the saying that is written, Death is swallowed up in victory.

"O death, where is thy sting? O grave, where is thy victory?"—*I Corinthians, 15:51-55.*

He felt just as sure as if he had been there and saw it happen, that his mother's grave had burst open when the Son of God made His appearance in midair and her body came forth a new body to be reunited with the soul. If only he had been ready and could have been caught up with her.

"My God," he choked, "I had strayed so far from Mother's teachings that I had become like many others. I did not believe that the Lord was really coming."

Bill ran out the door and into the street like a flash and looked both ways.

"Extra! Extra!" cried the newsboy.

With weak limbs that seemed they could not make the trip up the street, he rushed to get a paper.

With trembling hands and tears trickling down his cheeks, he clutched the paper and read about the great event—great for those who had gone, but terrible for those like Bill who had been left behind.

Bill saw picture after picture of those missing as he frantically turned the pages. Some he knew; others he did not know. What a feeling of horror Bill felt as he saw pictures of children from his section of town.

Gone! That word carried greater meaning than ever before. Bill tried to pray, but it was so hard for him to pray because he had not prayed in many a day, and the devil was there to taunt him for being left behind. After many efforts to pray, he finally gave up.

The people in Noah's day who refused to heed the call and find refuge in the ark found themselves outside the closed ark door and the judgments of God being poured out upon them. Now, like the people in Noah's day, the saints of God had been raptured and those left behind are in the Tribulation Period.

Bill rushed through the town to the cemetery to

his mother's last resting place. Breathlessly, he reached her grave, and with tears flowing down his cheeks like a river, he looked into an open grave. Mother had been resurrected, and he had failed to keep his promise.

People passed Bill on the left and right as he walked back to the main part of town. Some of them he knew, but he did not bother to speak. There wasn't anything to say. Men, women, boys, and girls, with astonishment on their countenance and fear written in their red-rimmed eyes, were talking excitedly to each other. Some stubbornly declared that they did not believe that the Son of God had come and that somebody was trying to play a prank; but facts were facts, and they could not be long denied. Too many loved ones had disappeared for anyone to do away with the fact that something drastic had happened.

Street cars clanged and clattered as they rocked cheerlessly on their way. Horns of motorists honked and people were in a mad rush hurrying—hurrying but going nowhere in particular. The people did not care whether they reached their work that morning or not. Why should they? All they had counted dear and had worked willingly for was so they could buy the luxuries of life, but now all their zeal and enthusiasm were gone. What an irksome feeling it would be, trying to work and thinking about going home to an empty house and the baby gone.

Bill had forgotten all about his store. Nothing seemed to matter now except he had missed the rapture. He never could have imagined that it would be like this just after the rapture took place.

A woman talking to the policeman on the corner lifted pleading eyes, begging him to help her find her husband. For once, Bill was glad he had no close loved ones. He used to become lonely, and many times he wished he had someone he could go home to after the day's work was done; but now he thinks how sad it would be to have had someone so dear and for them to be snatched from him as this woman's husband was snatched from her.

Bill thought of the war days and how terrible it was when the boys had to go away. He had gone to the station to see many of his close friends off, and he had consoled many a loved one's heart as the train pulled out; but this morning he has no consolation to give his friends and neighbors that were left behind. If only he could walk up to those mothers that are in great distress and give the great hope that their loved ones would come back, but he knows that he cannot do this. They were gone—caught away to be with the Lord forever.

CHAPTER IV

Mother Collins left Jim's house with a heavy heart Sunday afternoon. She had tried so hard to rescue Jim and Lucille, but she had failed.

"Oh, God," she prayed as she walked home, "is it on my part? Have I fallen short? Dear Father, show me the way to take. Lucille is so bitter against You, but please, God, forgive her. She doesn't realize what she is doing by rejecting You and putting a wonderful Redeemer like Your Son to scorn. Dear Father, give me words that will entice her to seek You. Help Jim to be strong and break away from the chains of the enemy."

She looked around about her and thought how good it was to know the Lord and not be in darkness as some were.

Every now and then a child passing greeted Mother Collins with a cheery, "Hello, Mother Collins."

All the children in her neighborhood for blocks knew her as Mother Collins. Their little voices were a consolation that afternoon and warmed her burdened heart. It would have been a great day for her if Jim and Lucille were saved.

Old Butch, her dog, waited anxiously for her. She took time to give him a gentle pat on the head before going into the house.

It was almost dinner time, but she did not want anything to eat, so she sat down at her reading table and opened God's Holy Word and began to read. Her thoughts were still on the morning message, so she began to turn to different passages of Scripture on the coming of the Lord.

"But I would not have you to be ignorant, brethren, concerning them which are asleep, that ye sorrow not, even as others which have no hope.

"For if we believe that Jesus died and rose again, even so them also which sleep in Jesus will God bring with him.

"For this we say unto you by the word of the Lord, that we which are alive and remain unto the coming of the Lord shall not prevent them which are asleep.

"For the Lord Himself shall descend from heaven with a shout, with the voice of the archangel, and with the trump of God: and the dead in Christ shall rise first:

"Then we which are alive and remain shall be caught up together with them in the clouds, to meet the Lord in the air: and so shall we ever be with the Lord.

"Wherefore comfort one another with these words."
—*I Thessalonians 4:13-18*.

What a wonderful feeling to know that Jesus would come one day and take away His own. As she turned the pages and read, she felt that the Lord must surely be coming soon.

"But ye, brethren, are not in darkness, that that day should overtake you as a thief.

"Ye are all the children of light, and the children

of the day: we are not of the night, nor of darkness."
—*I Thessalonians 5:4, 5.*

Yes, watch. That was what she had been trying to
do. Maybe in the near future her waiting and watching would be over then she would see Jesus.

Before closing the Bible, she turned to Luke 21:36
and read:

"Watch ye therefore, and pray always, that ye may
be accounted worthy to escape all these things that
shall come to pass, and to stand before the Son of
man."

With these words in her heart, she bowed before the
Lord and asked God to save Jim and Lucille. She
arose realizing that she must hurry because it would
soon be time for the evening service. After a quick
toilet and putting on her best bonnet, she left for
church, not knowing that it was the last time she
would be going to the house of God for service before
Jesus would come.

Someone stopped her outside the church and
wanted to talk, but she dismissed herself as quickly as
she dared without insulting her friend and made her
way to the prayer room and knelt in the presence of
the Creator of mankind. The minister had asked each
one to go to the prayer room and pray before the evening service. You could always expect those in a
lukewarm condition to neglect prayer. How could people have the Spirit of God and be so unconcerned about
the lost?

As she watched the crowd gathering for service,

she breathed a prayer to God that the Holy Spirit would have His way in the service that night. Some were standing on the outside laughing and talking, but on the inside shouts of victory and petitions were going up by some of the dear old saints in the prayer room.

Soon it was time for the service to begin. The singers filled the choir, but they did not know it was the last time before the rapture. It seemed to Mother Collins that she could feel the presence of the Lord greater than she had ever felt Him before. A holy atmosphere filled the building as the saints of God shouted the praises of God. They were not ashamed of their Lord.

What precious testimonies were given. Every one had been stirred by the message that morning, and each testimony was centered around the second coming of the Lord.

The messenger, Leo Maspero, arose; and before he preached, he directed a congregational song, "Our Lord is Coming Back to Earth Again." Verse after verse was sung, and it seemed to be lifted by angels and carried to the throne of God. The chorus of the song echoed and re-echoed with joy as they diligently sang.

After the congregational song, Leo Maspero began to read.

"Behold, I come as a thief. Blessed is he that watcheth, and keepeth his garments, lest he walk naked, and they see his shame."—*Revelation 16:15.*

Then, he began with another one of his great messages to warn the people that they were living in the last days and that the rapture was subject to take place at any time.

At this same hour in another section of the city, Dr. Morehead stood behind the sacred desk in a large cathedral speaking on the same subject but from a different angle. The group to whom he spoke was quite different from the group that was gathered at Fairview church. The Spirit of God was not prevalent, and the joy that comes from above was not in their midst. It was unusual for the house to be packed, for it was seldom that Dr. Morehead could get his congregation out to preaching services on Sunday evenings. His members wanted to play bridge, go to the movies, or to a dance. They enjoyed these things much better than going to church. The pastor did not care too much if they did not come but once a week (Sunday morning), because it gave him more time to play golf; and he did not have to think about some old, stuffy, musty sermon that he must preach. His pay came in just the same, and that was what he was there for.

Tonight, it was different. He really wanted to preach.

That fanatical evangelist, Leo Maspero, at Fairview had put in the paper that he would be speaking on "The Second Coming of the Lord." Dr. Morehead had been asked by some of his members what he thought about it, so he decided to announce that he would preach on the second coming also. Dr. Morehead's members had never heard him speak on the coming of the Lord, so, naturally, they could hardly wait for the evening service. Bridge parties were postponed, dances called off, and many other regular Sunday evening entertainments cancelled so they could hear what he had to say. They had heard many comments on the sermon that had been preached at Fairview church in the morning service, and they were alarmed.

The robed choir began to sing in their same old spirit and the congregation wriggled and turned impatiently waiting for them to finish. After all, they were interested in the message of the evening. Some came for curiosity's sake, and others felt a fear in their hearts from which they wanted to be free.

When the minister was ready to speak, many sat rigid in their seats. Some leaned a little forward. This was the most attention he had been given since he had come there more than twenty years ago to take over the pastorate after the death of The Reverend Thomas.

Dr. Morehead was thinking, as he entered the pulpit, of the condition of the church when he took it over. Reverend Thomas was a good man, but he had never had the chance of an education like Dr. Morehead. In ignorance, he had taught the people a lot of nonsense. After Dr. Morehead came along, he had erased a lot of that out of their minds. Some of them would not believe him no matter how much he talked to them and pointed out what the philosophers said about it, so they had gone to Fairview church to be with that noisy crowd. Oh well, if they wanted to be that narrow-minded and foolish, let them go. His church would get along better without them.

Tonight, he was very much annoyed to think his people, after sitting under his ministry all these years, could be stirred beyond words by some little upstart of a preacher who did not know what he was talking about. Some had even joined that crowd and embraced their doctrine on the second coming. Surely, this little preacher had not been away to college and studied under the great men of today.

He stuck his chest out a little farther as he thought, I will fix this group here tonight with that doctrine so they will feel foolish if they ever give it a second thought that the Lord is coming and catch people away—rapture them, as that group at Fairview calls it.

With a sneer on his lips and a hard gleam in his eyes, he began to speak. Everything was quiet and the audience listened attentively. Some sat with a look of satisfaction and confidence that their minister was wise and knew the ways of God and could tell them all about that rotten doctrine. Others felt a great fear clutching their hearts and wished that the minister would say he believed the Lord was coming one day and give them a chance to seek the Lord, but Dr. Morehead had no such idea in mind.

As he opened his message he said, "I am glad for the privilege to stand before this fine group of people tonight and tell you how damnable I think the doctrine on the second coming of the Lord is."

The old deacon, Eduard Abbey, shook his head with triumph and looked at Jake, with whom he had discussed the subject before service.

"I feel that God would have me to put your minds at ease, as you are His children and He does not want you to have unnecessary worries by believing a doctrine which the Bible does not teach. The Bible said false prophets would come, and that is surely what we have in a pulpit not so far from here.

"You may say, 'Dr. Morehead, what about those scriptures concerning His coming?'

"Well, many people do not realize that most of those scriptures are spiritual and not to be used in a literal sense at all. To tell you the truth, most of the Scripture is written to the Jews; therefore we Gentiles do not have to worry about them since they are written to the Jews only. I will admit that many of our ministers used to believe this doctrine, but that was when they did not have much education and did not have such opportunities of learning as we have today. This is a day of enlightenment, and no one should be in darkness.

"Now, do you think God would have us to be sad all the time? If I believed this doctrine that the Lord might come any time, I could not be happy, because I would have a great fear in my heart all the time. Intelligent people never believe such doctrine—only the feeble-minded."

Dr. Morehead smiled broadly when he said this, for out of the corner of his eye he was watching Vance

Day. He had heard him express his belief just before the service began, and he knew that Vance believed the Lord would come some day.

He and his wife, sitting in their regular pew, did not receive the statement as their pastor had intended. They did not seem embarrassed at the sarcastic remark that only the feeble-minded believed that the Lord was coming, because they had been taught the doctrine of the coming of the Son of God. He looked at his pastor with eyes of pity, and really deep down in his heart he felt sorry for him.

Vance had sat in this pew as long as he could remember; in fact, this was his grandmother's pew on his mother's side and her mother's before that. There had been Days in this church ever since it was built years ago.

As Vance sat there, his mind wandered back to his former pastor, Reverend Thomas, who used never to tire of talking about the coming of his Lord. One day he passed away and Vance stood by his bed just a few hours before the soul took its departure. Those precious lips that had given out God's Word so many times quoted these scriptures their last time in this life:

"For the Lord Himself shall descend from heaven with a shout, with the voice of the archangel, and with the trump of God and the dead in Christ shall rise first:

"Then we which are alive and remain shall be caught up together with them in the clouds, to meet the Lord in the air: and so shall we ever be with the Lord."—*I Thessalonians 4:16, 17.*

As he breathed these scriptures, you could see the glory of God shining on his face.

Tonight, Vance Day realized why he had sat back and not objected to Dr. Morehead's false doctrine against the second coming of the Lord. He had not rebuked him because he dreaded to have him turn scornful eyes upon him and count him among the fanatics.

Vance wondered how he could have denied his Lord and sat back and allowed his children and wife to hear such a false teaching. His mother died embracing the "blessed hope." It was true. Jesus was really coming for His saints.

The words that were falling from the minister's lips seemed like blasphemy. Vance Day felt the time had come for him to take his stand for his Lord. It was now or never, so he did something he had never done the many times he had attended services at his church. With determination written on their countenances, he and his wife arose to leave before the message was finished. The people looked at them in amazement. They had never seen a Day act that way. They had always seemed so holy. The whole congregation turned and looked after them and began nudging each other.

Dr. Morehead was bewildered, and he almost forgot what he was going to say next. Four or five others arose to follow the Days because they knew

where they were going. They were going to the
Fairview church!

Dr. Morehead tried to gather his wits enough to
finish the message. He wanted so much to pretend
that he had not noticed, but somehow he could never
manage to get himself under control and feel the self-
assurance that he felt at the first part of the message.

Finally, the service was dismissed and the outcome
of the meeting left some of them with a greater feeling of uneasiness.

The Days made a straight pathway to the Fairview
church. They could hear the singing, shouting, and
praises going up to God before they arrived at the
church.

The place was crowded, but they managed to
squeeze inside the door. The scene their eyes viewed
was different from that which they had just left. It
brought memories of the times when they used to
enjoy the blessings of the Lord in their church before
Dr. Morehead came to be their pastor. Their eyes
filled with tears as they beheld the glory of God shining on the faces of the saints as they sang praises
to God.

They arrived at the service in time to hear the
last song before the messenger arose to speak. Vance
Day noticed the same calm, sweet expression on the
young man's face that he used to see on Reverend
Thomas' face who had taught him the "blessed hope."
He spoke with assurance, and his dark brown eyes
sparkled with the glory of the God of mankind.

"I am happy to speak to this group on the coming of our Lord in these last days. It is nearer than ever before; and as we notice the signs of time, we know that it is near, even at the door. I am aware of the fact that many are not looking for Him. Some who claim to be His, are not really looking for Him to come.

"The Bible tells us: 'Behold, I come as a thief. Blessed is he that watcheth, and keepeth his garments, lest he walk naked, and they see his shame.'"—*Revelation 16:15.*

"Many are walking without the fear of God upon their lives. They are indulging in worldly pleasures of all kinds, seeking the amusements of this life, and not laying up treasures for the hereafter.

"I have been preaching for the last few nights from the Book of Daniel and the Book of Revelation. I hope these messages have stirred you Christian friends and given you a desire for a closer walk with the Master."

On and on the messenger of God spoke as if he had so much to tell the people and not much time in which to tell it. He gave scripture after scripture, and he did not seem to fear or shun any of God's Word.

Leo Maspero closed his message with: "Watch ye therefore, and pray always, that ye may be accounted worthy to escape all these things that shall come to pass, and to stand before the Son of man."—*Luke 21:36.*

Tonight was the first time Vance Day had wit-

nessed an old time altar service in many a day. He
felt the urge to run for the altar of prayer and renew
his covenant with the Lord.

The devil whispered, "What will the people think
about you? You have been a church member for
years. You are just excited and worked up. You
will be all right tomorrow. You have your job to
think about, and what will the members of your
church and your pastor think when they hear about
it?"

Vance Day did not wait to hear any more. He
rushed for the altar of prayer and his wife followed
him.

Hester Bell was astonished when she recognized
them walking down the aisle, for she knew they were
Dr. Morehead's members. Four or five more from
their church passed down the aisle on their way to
the altar also. Hester looked after them with fear
and trembling and wished she dared do what they and
Nancy had done; then she decided she would wait
until another time.

That night, after Hester went home, she lay awake
a long time thinking about the many things she had
learned that day. It was wonderful to know that
Jesus was coming if one was ready, but it was an awful
feeling when one was not ready.

As Hester tossed to and fro and could not go to
sleep, her mother, in a downstairs bedroom, lay wide
awake meditating upon the coming of the Lord. She
had not answered when Hester tiptoed to her door

and gently called her when she came from church, because she did not feel that she could stand to hear more about the coming of the Lord. Frank Wilson lay by her side sleeping soundly. She tried to breathe a prayer as she lay there in the dark, but she could not put words together to make sentences. Finally, she decided she would go to the next church service and get right with the Lord. Surely, the Lord would not come before then.

CHAPTER V

Hester awoke with a start. The sun was beaming in her window and all seemed strangely quiet. Cold sweat lay on her brow. She had been having a horrible dream. She dreamed she was in the Tribulation Period and the bottomless pit was opened and those horrible looking animals the preacher told about, in the Book of Revelation, came forth. They had faces as faces of men, hair as hair of women and teeth as teeth of lions, just as the preacher had said they would. One of those terrible looking locusts had just about overtaken her when she woke up.

She lay still a moment, so thankful to be awake and know that it was only a dream. She heard the birds singing in the Australian Pines just outside the window and a cart jostling down the street. She thought it must be Ben, the vegetable peddler.

Then, it happened! Like a thunderbolt from the skies, a newsboy rushed excitedly down the street in front of Hester's home shouting the shocking news.

"Extra! Extra! Thousands of people disappeared around six o'clock this morning! Extra! Extra! Read all about it!"

Hester almost lost consciousness. The bed seemed to be going around and around, and then the room joined in and things were getting blacker and blacker. She fought desperately to keep from fainting. The Lord had come! It was not a dream but a dreadful reality and she had been left behind!

"My God!   No, I just can't be left behind!"

Only last night she had been in church with Nancy. At the thought of Nancy her heart almost stopped. Nancy just could not be gone.   Nancy was her closest friend and had always stood up for her when others failed.   She walked to school with her every morning and they were in the same classes.   She just could not bear to ever go to that classroom again and look across at that empty seat where Nancy used to sit.   She could see her blond hair and pink cheeks and the wonderful smile on her face after God had saved her last night.   A dear friend like that just could not be gone.

By this time, the newsboy was a block down the street and he was still shouting, "Extra!   Extra!   Thousands of people have disappeared!"

Hester pinched herself and tried shaking herself to make sure that she was not dreaming.   Oh, if she would only wake up and find it to be a bad dream, she would give anything she ever owned.   In her heart, she felt if the rapture had not really taken place, she would get Nancy and they would go to Mother Collins' house and ask her to help her find the Lord.   If anyone ever knew the Lord, Hester felt Mother Collins did.

Shaking as Belshazzar did when the hand wrote on the wall, she managed to get out of bed.   How she got into her robe she never knew.   A lump was in her throat and she could not swallow.   She wanted to cry but not one tear would come.   She was as one in a trance. Her hands moved, but they felt as if they were not a part of her.

Her mother and daddy's room was at the foot of the stairs. She pounded madly on the door, and before her mother awoke enough to answer, she threw the door wide open and jumped in the bed with them too much excited to speak. Susan sat up in bed, rubbing her eyes with amazement, and Frank awoke with a start. They knew something dreadful had happened. What, they did not know.

Many things crowded the minds of Susan and Frank as Hester lay there staring at them and trembling from head to toe. They thought maybe the house was on fire, a burglar had gotten in and many other thoughts came to their minds, but neither of them gave a thought as to what had really happened.

As Hester lay there, she felt as if she must be dying. Her hands were numb and clammy, and her tongue seemed twice its thickness.

At last, she was able to speak.

"It's happened! It's happened! The Lord's come! The Lord's come! They are gone! Thousands of people are gone! I tell you, the rapture has taken place!"

Susan Wilson stared at her daughter in unbelief, and with a gentle pat on the shoulder she tried to quiet her. She tried to laugh, but the muscles in her face froze. Frank thought it was some fantastic something Hester had dreamed up. She was good on creating excitement.

With a portentous, hollow voice he began to speak.

"Hester, I just feel like spanking the daylights out of you for coming in here disturbing my rest like this. Your mother will be nervous the rest of the day. I know where you heard that nonsense. I have been hearing the fellows down at the pool room telling about some of the unheard of things that evangelist at Fairview church is preaching. They think he should be run out of town, and I, for one, am ready to help do it. I forbid you to go back to that church again. Do you understand!" he thundered.

"Frank, you are beside yourself. You have never spoken to Hester like this before. She did not mean any harm I am sure. It is not a fantastic story that the Lord is really coming some day, but He has not come yet. I know that Hester has just been dreaming," she said trying to calm both of them. "After listening to the messages on the coming of the Lord, she thought it was real. I will admit she gave me an awful scare for a moment, but I will be all right now."

"Hester, darling," Susan continued, "go on back to your room and get dressed. This is school morning you know."

Hester had not expected this reaction from her parents, and with the shock of hearing the newsboy and now this unusual outburst from her father, it left her dumbfounded. Finally, she managed to speak again, and this time the tears that had refused to come before began to flow. As a dam holds the waters back until the floodgate is opened, so it was with Hes-

ter. This was unusual for Hester and alarming to her
parents. She was shaking all over like a leaf in a
mighty storm.

"I tell you it is so. Oh, how I wished it was a
fancy of mine, but it has really happened. I heard the
newsboy shouting it as he rushed down the street a
few minutes ago. I know it is so and we have been
left behind."

Hester threw her hands in the air and gave a pitiful
scream. Susan Wilson began to tremble all over. Her
face paled, and with pleading eyes, she looked at her
daughter and then at her husband.

"Frank," she choked, "you don't suppose the child
is right, do you?"

"Of course not," he answered impatiently. "Don't
tell me you, too, are getting a crazy notion like that.
We will all be in the asylum for the insane if this
keeps up. Now turn on the radio. It is about time
for the seven o'clock news, and I want you both to
get yourselves under control."

With an unsteady hand, Susan reached out and
turned the button on the little white radio beside
her bed.

"FLASH! THE GREATEST TRAGEDY AND
SHOCK TO EVER REACH THE AMERICAN SHORES
CAME THIS MORNING AROUND SIX O'CLOCK.
THOUSANDS OF PEOPLE DISAPPEARED INTO
THIN AIR. IT IS THE MOST UNBELIEVABLE
THING THAT MANKIND HAS EVER HAD TO FACE.
ALL THE SMALL CHILDREN ARE GONE IN THIS

CITY. CALLS ARE COMING IN FROM OTHER CITIES AND IT IS THE SAME EVERYWHERE. MANY ADULTS ARE GONE, TOO. IN SOME HOMES IT IS JUST THE FATHER, THE MOTHER, A DAUGHTER OR SON; THEN THERE ARE SOME ENTIRE FAMILIES GONE. WE ARE BAFFLED BY THIS GREAT MYSTERY. SOME ARE SAYING THE LORD HAS COME AND CAUGHT HIS SAINTS AWAY. I DO NOT KNOW WHAT HAS HAPPENED, BUT I DO KNOW THAT PEOPLE ARE REALLY GONE. STAY TUNED TO THIS STATION FOR LATEST DEVELOPMENTS."

The Wilsons were petrified and not able to move until the news commentator finished. Susan's eyes were glued to the radio, and at the close of the news, she let out a doleful cry and fell postrate on the floor.

Frank Wilson pulled himself out of the bed and fell down on his knees with his head buried in his hands. He began to pray for the first time in his life. He had always thought he could not pray if he had to, for he did not think he would know how to talk to a being like God; but now he found no difficulty in forming a prayer.

"My God, my God, this incredible thing just can't be so. Please have mercy on us and don't let it be so. I have sinned against You, and I know I have no right to ask this of You, but please don't let it be. Oh, God, it just can't be! It just can't be!" he cried. Don't forget us! Oh, God, please don't forget us!"

It was odd to see Frank Wilson act in this manner.

He was never one to recognize God in whatever he decided to do. He lived each day as if there were no God who had made the universe in which he lived.

Hester's body shook with sobs, and it did not help her any to see her father cry and pray to God as he was doing. Oh, if he would have sought the face of God like this before the Christ of God had come, it might have been a different story for all of them. Now, it was too late. It had happened and they had all been left behind. Why didn't she get ready last night! She would not be here this morning, but she would be hidden away with the Lord somewhere. How foolish she had been. She had gambled with her soul and lost it. The passage of escape from the Tribulation Period was closed. Only last night it was open, but she turned it down, not realizing what it would mean to seek for the passage and find it closed.

The messenger who preached last night on the "blessed hope" was gone. Mother Collins was gone, and all those other saints were gone, too. Never could she go to a service like she was in last night and hear the songs of Zion, the testimonies of God's people and hear them tell about the "blessed hope."

An empty feeling filled her heart as she thought of the people she counted dearest in all the world being gone. She had never known how much she loved the people at the Fairview church until now. Now they were gone and Nancy with them—or was Nancy gone?

A desire seized her to rush to Nancy's house and find out whether Nancy were really gone. Hester felt she could bear it much better if Nancy was not gone.

As she made her exit through the back door, she did not bother to close it. Down the street she ran toward Nancy's house.

The trees, with their beautiful branches making a green canopy over her head, did not seem to play any part in her thoughts today as they usually did. When she finally came in sight of Nancy's house sitting tall and white back from the main road, with the beautiful shrubbery and flower beds here and there, it did not give Hester a thrill as it always had. This morning, all the beauty was gone.

All the sunshine in her life had vanished, and one thought stood out utmost in her mind. The rapture had taken place around six o'clock. While she slept it had happened.

Nancy's mother was in the kitchen. This was unusual for Kate Cline seldom did any cooking. Why was she in the kitchen and where was Hannah, the maid?

Mrs. Cline looked very much annoyed when Hester almost ran into her in her rush. Hester was panting for breath, and one could scarcely understand what she was saying.

"Wh-er-e is Nan-cy?" she stammered.

Mrs. Cline started to give her a rebuke for rushing into the house with such disrespect, but she stopped short as she saw a look on Hester's face she had never witnessed before.

"Nancy is still in bed. Land's sake, Hester, what

has happened to you, child? I have never seen you so upset."

Hester tried hard to control herself and speak with calmness, but that was impossible with the strain she was under.

"Mrs. Cline, don't you know what has happened? The Lord came about six o'clock and caught people away."

Mrs. Cline stared incredulously. She knew something dreadful must have happened because of Hester's discomposure. Great fear seized her heart.

Then she thought of Hannah, her maid. She had not come to work. Hannah was always on time or let her know why she would be late, but there had not been a call and she had not shown up for work.

Hannah was a great one to believe that some day the Lord would come as a thief in the night and take away His jewels. Many times she had told her mistress about it, over her protest. It was just as natural for Hannah to talk about her Lord as it was for water to run down hill.

She always ended the conversation after they had talked about the Lord with: "You better get ready. It will be too late after it has happened."

Hester did not wait for more. She rushed up the stairs and knocked on Nancy's door. She listened, scarcely daring to breathe and hoping against hope that she would hear Nancy's sleepy hello.

Just then, Nancy's mother, out of breath from

climbing the stairs, said, "Open the door and see if she is all right."

Hester opened the door and stared at an empty bed. Nancy was gone! Mrs. Cline could not believe her eyes as she looked over Hester's shoulder. Why, Nancy could not be gone! Why should Nancy be gone and Hester left behind if the Lord had come?

"Hester," Kate nervously spoke, "where do you suppose she is? She has never acted like this before."

Hester turned tortured eyes upon her and said, "She is hidden away somewhere with the Lord just as the minister told us it would be last night. Nancy took heed; now she is with the Lord. I waited, thinking I had plenty of time, and now I have been left behind!"

"What do you mean?" Kate questioned anxiously.

Hester realized for the first time that Kate had probably already gone to bed when Nancy came in last night, and that Nancy had not told the great news of her conversion to her mother; now she would never tell her.

"Mrs. Cline, Nancy found the Lord last night. She tried to get me to go to the altar with her, but something seemed to hold me back; and I thought I would wait and think it over a little longer. My God, how I wish I had gone. I know it must have been a wonderful feeling to have been caught away to be with the Lord."

Just then, they heard the newsboy shouting the

dreadful truth. "Thousands of people disappeared around six o'clock this morning."

Kate pulled the curtain back and stared through the sparkling windowpane to the street where the newsboy was standing. She was not crying. She was too shocked to cry. If only she could cry it would be a great relief. It was hammering like mad in her brain that the Lord had come and Nancy was gone with Him.

"What a fool I have been. Many times Hannah talked with me and showed me Scriptures to prove what she said, but I hardened my heart against it. I tried to make myself believe that Hannah did not have much education and did not understand the Scriptures. Now Hannah is gone!"

Hannah had had a hard time in life and had to earn her living as a servant. Kate had always pitied Hannah before, but this morning she would give ten thousand worlds if she could change places with her. After all, Hannah had been far richer than she, and she, Kate Cline, knew it not.

To look at the trees and the birds fluttering here and there in the warm spring sunshine, one would think all was peaceful, but all the peace and happiness had fled and left disaster.

Kate Cline thinks of the times she could have gone to the house of God, but she was always too busy. She makes a pathetic picture as she stands there reminiscing her past, not moving a muscle or saying a word.

Hester started to say something to Kate, but she changed her mind. She turned suddenly and hurried from the room. She must get away from this terrifying scene.

As she rushed through the kitchen, a cold, icy hand pressed her throat as she thought of Hannah, the maid, being gone. Could she never forget that the rapture had taken place? It seemed everywhere she looked there was something to remind her that the Lord had come.

CHAPTER VI

When Jim came in from the drugstore with the sleeping tablets, he stopped by the nursery. As he viewed the room, he had to choke back the tears. It was just as Baby Sue had left it the night before. Toys were scattered here and there, and a teddy bear lay on the pillow. A little arm had been lying across it when the Lord came. Sue always had to have her teddy bear before she would go to sleep.

"My God, why weren't Lucille and I ready to go? We should all be together this morning."

Jim closed the nursery door to shut out the scene that had always been so dear. This morning, it sent pains through his heart. It hurt like nothing had ever hurt before.

He heard Lucille moaning in their bedroom. He must forget his sorrow for the time being and try to comfort his wife.

Again and again she would look up at Jim with tortured eyes and beg so pitifully for her baby. No matter what he tried to tell Lucille, he could not comfort her. He would be willing to surrender his life if he could give her baby back to her, but he knew he could never bring their child back. God had given her to them, and the Lord had a right to take her if He wanted to.

It seemed to Jim a long time before he finally got Lucille to sleep. Their friends had been calling, and about the time she was almost asleep, the telephone would ring and rouse her. They were so humble now and men that Jim had never been able to feature crying had broken down and cried as if their hearts would break. It was maddening! If they would only stop calling. Didn't they understand they had enough sorrow of their own without being told of other's sorrows?

After an endless eternity, the telephone ceased ringing, and Lucille was sleeping the sleep of the weary and exhausted. Jim looked down at her, and she looked like a child as she lay there with a tear on each cheek. Those tears reminded him of the tears that had been shed by his mother for her lost boy. His mother had shed many tears that he might find the Lord, but they had fallen in vain; and he was left behind to be in the Tribulation Period.

He tiptoed softly from the room, choking back the tears, and went into the living room and turned the radio on low to one of the local stations. The usual morning program was not on as all the time on the programs was given to reports of the rapture. It was so strange to sit there and listen to the rapture being talked about as something that had already taken place. Jim had heard it discussed all his life as an event for the future, but now the news reporter was giving some eyewitness stories of some that were with their loved ones and friends when it took place—reports of train wrecks, ships at sea left without a pilot or captain, airplanes crashing because the pilot had disappeared and there was no end of bus and car wrecks.

Jim flipped the button off on the radio and walked slowly to the door, opened it as one in a trance, and stepped out on the front porch. The street looked painfully familiar and yet strange. People were racing here and there. Jim could detect the excitement on their countenances from a distance. Some were running, some walking at a fast pace, and others were walking very slowly as in a daze. Men and women rushed down the street with tears streaming down their cheeks, but they did not appear to be ashamed.

As Jim looked upon these people, he forgot his own sorrow and yearned to comfort these people that were in great distress.

Just then, a group of people passed and one was yelling, "Let's go to Fairview church. Dr. Morehead is going to explain what has happened!"

Jim did not need anyone to explain to him what had happened, because he knew too much about it now. It would have been bad enough to have been left behind and not have known the right way, but to be left behind after being taught the right way and what to expect was almost more than Jim could bear. He decided to follow the crowd and see what Dr. Morehead would have to say now. He had not believed nor preached the Lord's return, so what would be his theory now?

When Jim reached the church that he had attended so many times with his mother, the rapture having taken place became a greater reality. He had seen his mother sit in the second pew on the right for many years, but a stranger was sitting there this morning.

Jim's eyes scrutinized the faces of the crowd. Some he knew; others he did not know. Jim knew many of these people had hated his mother's church and its way of worship. They had persecuted the church, but now they were there with pale, drawn faces, like doomed men that were waiting for the death sentence.

A hush came over the audience as the speaker took his place behind the sacred desk. He stood pale and haggard, and he looked as if he had been on a drunk. His eyes were red-rimmed, and anyone could see that he had been crying. He had cried until he could not cry any more.

Dr. Morehead's wife discovered about eight o'clock that their child was missing, and she called the police; but they informed her that there were hundreds of babies missing, as well as adults. He could not believe it at first; but facts were facts, and it had to become a reality.

Previous to this time, he could stand in the pulpit and tell people that the rapture was just an old-fogyish idea that someone had thought up and that the Bible did not mean that the Lord would actually come one day. Now, it was different. His own child was gone, and he and the people he had deceived had been left behind.

The eyes of some of Dr. Morehead's members sitting in the congregation seemed to burn his flesh. He started to speak; but his voice choked, and he burst into tears. This brought fresh tears to the eyes of many that were suffering from the loss of a loved one. Finally, he managed to speak with a weak, trembling voice. A sepulcher quietness fell over the huge crowd as he began to confess.

"Men and brethren, I have been a fool. Yes, I have been a blind fool. The Bible tells us if the blind lead the blind they will all fall into the ditch. I had never reaized what this statement meant until this morning. If it had not been for me, some of you would be out of this hell of torture that you are in right now. Believe me, friends," he paused for a moment, "if I might call you my friend,"

Just then Jane Sloan stood to her feet toward the back of the building and shouted at the speaker.

"Friends! Indeed! after all the lies you have told us! You were supposed to be our spiritual leader whom we could depend on to lead us right and instruct us in the ways of the Lord. We believed you when you said it was nonsense to believe that the Lord was coming, but it has happened!" she screamed hysterically. "Our children are gone and we have been left behind. You deceiver! You blasphemer! Maybe you are satisfied since you have damned our souls! You are no friend of ours, but you have been used as an instrument of the devil to rob us of our souls!"

Someone took hold of Jane's arm and pulled her down in the seat before she had a chance to say more. If only he could have shouted to this crowd of people and told them it was a false accusation that the woman was making, but she was one of his members and he had led her wrongly. What Jane said was true, so what could he do?

"My God! Have mercy!" he cried. "I know what has been said is true. I see it all now. Believe me, when I say I would give ten thousand worlds like this one if I could right this wrong that I have done. I had a good Christian mother who told me this would happen some day. When I went away to college, I drank in their rotten doctrine, ate their disbelief of the Bible and the Virgin Birth, and here I am left behind. I thought it was up-to-date and sophisticated, and I went back home feeling that I knew more than my old-fashioned mother. I tried to tell her, but she would not listen; and thank God she did not because she would be left behind as I am. I stopped going to visit her, because I was ashamed of her ignorance, as I called it. Now, she is gone. I just came from her house before coming here, and I know she is gone."

The tears were blinding his vision of the sea of faces before him, but he must go on. There was so much he must say.

"One of my members, Vance Day, walked out during my message last night because I was denying the second coming of the Lord. This morning, when I realized my child was gone, I rushed over to his house to try to rectify myself. I discovered he and his wife were both gone.

"We may just as well face the facts. The Lord has come, just as the Bible said He would. There are different theories about all these thousands of people disappearing, but don't be deceived any longer. The Lord has really come and taken His children away.

"I allowed the devil to deceive me. There were times it worried me, and I could not get away from the thought that Jesus was coming; but I kept telling myself that it was just uneducated people who believed such a story and that erudite men that taught me in college could not be wrong. Finally, after many days of struggling with this, I convinced myself that the doctrine of the coming of the Son of God was all wrong, and my mind was set free.

"This morning, I am reminded of Second Thessalonians, two, eleven and twelve. 'And for this cause God shall send them strong delusion, that they should believe a lie:

"'That they all might be damned who believe not the truth, but had pleasure in unrighteousness.'

"It does not matter what anyone might try to tell me, I know now that the Bible means just what it says. My God! why did I let the devil deceive me as I did?" he ruefully said.

Many of his members wept with him. They could not blame him altogether, because they had been taught by their pastor before him that the coming of the Lord would take place sometime. They did not have to believe what he taught them. They could have left their church and gone to Fairview as others from their congregation had done.

Those who had not been taught the second coming of Jesus, looked at Dr. Morehead with hatred in their eyes, and they felt a great honor would be bestowed upon their city to rid it of a man like this.

He started to say more, then paused. After all, what could he say now to make amends to those whom he had deceived? He stumbled blindly out of the pulpit from which so many of God's ministers had heralded the "blessed hope" of the second coming of Jesus. Today, they were not here because they had been caught away to be with their Lord.

Down the aisle he moved, and insulting words floated to his ears. Weak and trembling, he finally reached the door and passed into the street. How he got home he never knew, but he fell on his face in the parlor and wept.

"My God, if only I had believed Thy Word. Thousands have lived in darkness and are left behind because of ministers like me."

In the midst of the crowd at Fairview church sat Mary Conway, a dark blue-eyed girl of about fifteen years of age. This was not a strange place to her, because she had attended this church all her life and had been taught the second coming of the Lord; but never did she think she would come here sometime under these circumstances.

Mary's mother and father had been faithful members of the church and had won many souls for the Lord. Mary believed that the Lord would come sometime, but although she had heard the second coming preached all her life, she never thought that it would happen in her day. She intended to get right with the

Lord, but she felt she was young and had a lot of time to think about serving the Lord. The second coming of the Lord had been preached for years, and she thought this doctrine would, no doubt, be preached many more years before the Lord would actually come.

On Sunday night, Mary felt the Spirit of the Lord dealing with her heart as it had never dealt before. Once, conviction was so strong she almost yielded, but she kept waiting, until finally the altar invitation came to a close, and there she was still standing back. Mary lived all this over again as she sat there in the house of God.

Strangers sat in the pews that had long been occupied by dear old saints of God who loved the Lord with all their hearts. Sitting beside these strangers were some of the members and friends of Fairview.

Mary would give ten million worlds if she could only live the night before over. Instead of being there, she would be hidden away with the Lord. Why should such a catastrophe be hers?

As Mary sat in the dimly lighted building, it seemed she had lived years since the night before. The scene of the family altar, her father reading from the soft, black, leather-covered Bible, and her mother placing a warm kiss on her cheek before turning out the light were very vivid now.

Monday morning Mary had awaked with a start and sat up in bed. All was tranquil and still. She glanced at the clock to see that it was half past eight.

"Why this is school morning! I wonder why mother

hasn't called? She never lets me oversleep. This is my last year in high school, and if I miss a day I'll . . . ."

She slid out of bed and hurried into her negligee. There must be something wrong, she thought, so she rushed to the kitchen almost shouting, "Mother! Mother!"

There was no sound of dishes rattling nor the appearance of anyone's being near. A strange atmosphere filled the house. Standing in the kitchen door, she glanced from one side to the other, but her mother was not there. The stove was red hot, but nothing was on the burners cooking. There was flour in the pan, and yes, the dough was partly made.

"Mother never leaves things like this," she anxiously said to herself. "Maybe she left a note in the living room."

She looked on top of the radio where her mother always left notes when necessary, but there was no sign of one.

Maybe mother and daddy have been called out to pray for someone sick, she thought. Why haven't I thought of this before and saved myself all this worry? Her mother and father were called out many times in the early morning hours to pray and minister to the sick, but they had always called her before leaving or left a note. Probably, she thought, she left in such a hurry she forgot it, or she planned to be back before it was time for me to get up.

There was nothing for Mary to do but wait, as it

was too late to try to get to school on time. She switched the radio on and dialed her favorite station, WXZX; then picking up a Life magazine, she sat down to read and listen.

Suddenly, it came like a bomb had burst.

"At six o'clock this morning, thousands of people disappeared," the news reporter was saying. "It is a great mystery. There have been many solutions given by many people, but it seems that no one theory will satisfy. The latest news bulletin that the Lord has come and caught them up in the sky seems to have been accepted by the majority of the people."

The color drained from Mary's face, her pulse quickened, and she began to breathe rapidly and unevenly.

Could this be a story, she thought. Was this a news report, and had thousands of people really disappeared? Dozens of thoughts penetrated her mind.

"It can't be!" she sharply said aloud, "but it upsets me and makes me jittery to hear something like this. It must be an introduction to a story."

The news reporter was going on, giving more detailed reports and reading a list of names of some of the people who had disappeared. When he read Marion Stelson and Mother Collins' name, she became frenzied, and things began to get black before her. This was no time to faint, but was she going to?

Only last night Mary had seen these dear old saints of God shouting and praising God. If they were gone, surely the rapture must have taken place.

How she ever made it to the front door she never knew. As she stood in the front door, she stared wildly up and down the street. People were running here and there. Some were hysterically crying as they passed the house; others were praying.

The newsboy was crying, "Extra! Extra! Thousands of people disappeared around six o'clock this morning!"

That's where mother and daddy are! The Lord has come! she thought. Giving a shrill scream, she fell in a faint. After a few minutes, she slowly opened her eyes and looked at the ceiling.

Pulling herself up, she screamed, "Oh, my Lord! You have come and left me behind! What shall I do? My mother and daddy are gone, and I'm all alone!"

It just did not seem that it could be true. Only last night she was at church with all the saints; and the messenger talked about the coming of the Lord as a future event, but now it was a thing of the past.

Swiftly her figure moved into the street and joined the fast, heavy footsteps of the hundreds of remorseful souls. Going where? They did not exactly know. They were going anywhere to keep on the move and ease their torture.

Mary was going to see if the saints were really gone. Oh, if it could only be a mistake. Mary knocked on door after door, trying to find just one member of the church she thought would have been ready if the Lord had come. There was not a true saint of God to be found.

The hot tears blinded her eyes so she could not see the way she was going, and the heavy load that was upon her heart was almost more than she could bear. It seemed she was in a mighty hurricane and all her loved ones had been swept away. It would be a relief for death to come and take her, but she could not die with just a desire.

As the crowd rushed madly toward the church, Mary followed. Through curiosity she went to the church just to hear what Dr. Morehead had to say. He had opposed them bitterly. What would he say now? Would he still say that those teachings were hatched up by a group of fanatics, or would he be honest and admit that the Bible is true?

Dr. Morehead was a different man, and he looked different as he stood before the great throng of people. He used to fight God's people and still claim to be on the Lord's side. Mary always felt that people of that kind were the greatest hurt to the Kingdom of God.

This morning, she listened attentively to his speech. He was a pathetic picture as he stood before that great crowd making his confession. Yes, that was really what it was. At last, this man realized the truth of God's Word and knew he had been deceived. Mary felt sorry for him. He had done wrong, terribly wrong, but now he was confessing his wrong. She knew his confession would not help some, because he had been the object of their deceit.

As she observed the faces of the people, she saw

torture and pain in their eyes. They were asking themselves why he did not tell them those things instead of keeping them in darkness until now and then want them to forgive him?

At last, all the people were gone and Mary was left to herself and her thoughts. Life did not seem worth living. In her imagination she could visualize the saints of God gathered there for service and hear them shouting and singing praises to God. If they were only there today, she realizes she would gladly rush to the altar of prayer and get saved, but it is too late now. She never dreamed she would miss them as she did then.

Jim left the church with a heavy heart. He had not been told anything new, because he knew that the Lord had come. It did not matter what anyone might say. He knew beyond a doubt that the rapture had taken place.

He walked along the street thinking of how happy his mother and daddy must be this morning after being separated so long. His mother had always longed for this time; at last it had come. He could have been with them, but he had failed to heed the call of the Spirit.

Jim passed by Joe's grocery, but it was closed. Joe had been a real soldier of the cross; he did not let business come before the work of his Lord. He remembered how Joe would tell the customers to hurry because it was service night and he wanted to get to church on time. He was not wrapped up in the material things of life; but he was seeking a city whose builder and maker is God, so he was ready when the Lord came.

Bread had been left at the door by the bread man, but Joe had sold his last loaf of bread the day before. Milk and vegetables were stacked beside the bread, but Joe had no use for them now.

Hot, salty tears flooded Jim's eyes as he remembered the many times Joe had tried to persuade him to surrender to the Lord. Now, he knew he would never mention the name of the Lord to him again. How could he have passed up so many opportunities to have prepared?

CHAPTER VII

When Hester arrived back home from Nancy's house, she found her mother in a hysterical condition and her daddy still praying and crying. She longed to tell them that Nancy was gone, but they were in such an upset condition, she knew it would be some time before she could mention it.

How fortunate Nancy was to have gotten ready to meet the Lord the night before He came. Hester could have gotten ready, too, for the Spirit had dealt forcefully with her heart; but she had rejected Him.

What about all those people that were in that service and had rejected the Lord just as she had done? Hester knew some of them had once known the Lord, but they had let the devil cheat them out of their experience, and now they were left behind.

It was terrifying enough for anyone to be left behind, Hester thought, but for someone to have once known the Lord and then be left behind was more horrifying. How she wished she had gone to the altar last night, but now it was too late. The regrets were there just as the minister had said, only many times worse. No one could describe the eerie feeling and the remorse she felt. It was so terrible it did not seem that it could be real, but she knew it was because the newsboys were screaming it on every street corner; and there was the established fact that Nancy was gone and Hannah had not showed up for work.

Was Mother Collins gone? She decided she would do some investigating.

As she raced up the street, she passed haggard people with pale, drawn faces. Some were crying and screaming; some sat dejected on the edge of the sidewalk with a petrified stare. She tried to avert the poignant scenes, but the doleful cries could not be locked out.

It seemed ages before she reached Mother Collins' home, but at last she came to the white picket fence surrounding the little bungalow. Butch met her at the gate with a joyous bark, wagging his bushy tail. Sorrow was written in his eyes as if he were deeply worried.

The door was standing open. Maybe Mother Collins was there after all, and it was a mistake about the rapture.

She called loudly, "Mother Collins! Mother Collins!" but all was still.

The clock ticking on the mantel in the living room sent weird chills up and down her spine. Butch nestled close to her legs and gave a bound into the house, looking behind him as if he were bidding her to follow. Trembling, she stepped inside the door. The same strange atmosphere she had felt in Nancy's room was there also. She stood in the middle of the living room and looked around. Everything was spic-and-span just like Mother Collins always kept it. How long she stood there she did not know.

Butch brought her to her senses by barking furiously from Mother Collins' bedroom. Maybe she was sick. It is strange how people will try to have hope when really there is none.

What she saw, as she entered the bedroom, almost took her breath away. She was viewing the same scene Jim had witnessed only a few hours before. As her eyes took in the order of the room, she knew without a doubt that the rapture had surely taken place. There were Mother Collins' shoes, clothes, and glasses lying on the floor by the side of the bed. The tears rolled slowly down her cheeks, and she remembered the conversation she had had with Mother Collins only yesterday afternoon as they had walked home together from church. It had been only a matter of hours from then until the rapture would have really taken place.

As Hester stood there in Mother Collins' bedroom, she never realized the wonderful experience Mother Collins had passed through in that room around six o'clock that morning. About five-thirty, she arose not realizing that the last morning she would get out of bed before the rapture would have taken place had come . The burden for Jim and Lucille was so heavy on her heart, and the coming of the Lord seemed so near.

After praying and pouring her heart out to God, she arose with a song in her heart and rejoiced as she thought of the great number of souls that had found the Lord in the night service.

As she was making up the bed, she was thinking

of the joys and the heartaches of life and how the Lord had always stood by his people. Then, she began to sing the old hymn, "I'm in the Glory Land Way."

All of a sudden, the room was lighted up with the glory of God, and a loud voice cried, "Behold, the bridegroom cometh; go ye out to meet Him." Her heart leaped with joy. She heard the shout of her Lord, and then she felt something touch her body, and the most soothing feeling she had ever felt ran through her. The change had come. In a moment, in the twinkling of an eye, she was changed. She felt herself being lifted, and through the air she sailed. She heard the voices of the saints of God praising their Redeemer as they were caught up. Their voices sounded like the voice of many waters.

She, with the thousands of others, could cry out, "Oh, glorious morn. Oh, grave, where is thy victory? Oh, death, where is thy sting?"

Death had been swallowed up in victory. They were caught away to be with their Lord forever.

Hester turned and left the room hurriedly. She wanted to get away from the heart-rending scene. It would haunt her the rest of her life.

As she entered the living room, she spied the open Bible on the reading desk, and she seemed to be drawn to it. She read the same verse of Scripture that Jim had read. "Therefore be ye also ready: for in such an hour as ye think not the Son of man cometh."— *Matthew 24:44* Cold sweat covered her body. That was a message straight from heaven warning people to get ready. Now it had happened, and thousands like herself had been left behind.

Butch nestled up close to Hester, and she stooped down and patted him gently saying: "She is gone old boy. I know it is hard to believe and hard to understand, but it is so. Don't sorrow for her, Butch."

Hester was talking to Butch as if he were human.

"She lived and waited for this time. That was the main theme of her conversation. I am sure she is happy with Him this morning."

Hester looked up into the blue and tried to visualize the joy and peace Mother Collins was surely enjoying at that moment, but tears filled her eyes and shut out the view of the blue above. Blindly, she stumbled down the steps. It seemed she would die if she stayed there another minute.

As she walked up the street, she heard someone crying. It was a woman's voice, but who was it? Crying was a familiar sound now, but that person was crying unusually loud. Just then, she saw someone sprawled on the front steps of Mrs. Pickett's house sobbing. Hester rushed up the walk to the figure. As she drew near, she saw that it was Mrs. Pickett. Hester spoke to her, but she did not answer. After many attempts to get her attention, she came out of her hysteria and looking up cried, "You blessed child! You, too, have been left behind."

"Oh, Mrs. Pickett, are some of your loved ones gone?" Hester asked anxiously.

"No, it isn't that some of my loved ones were

caught away, but you remember my daughter Hazel that nurses in the Rheims Hospital?"

"Uh-hum," Hester answered.

"She was taking care of the nursery when the rapture took place. They said she was standing in the middle of the nursery room when every baby in the room disappeared. She looked around, and there wasn't a cry from any of the cribs. Upon examining them, she found that every baby in the nursery had vanished. She did not know what to make of it. She knew no one could have come in and gotten the babies. They had disappeared into thin air.

"She became hysterical and began screaming for dear life. Some of the nurses rushed to her. They knew something dreadful had happened to make Hazel act like that, because she was always so calm in time of emergencies. They tried to calm her, and after working with her for sometime, she became quiet and told them how the babies had vanished into thin air. At first, they did not believe her, and they began to wink at each other, because they thought she was losing her mind. She insisted it was so, so they began to search for the babies, and sure enough they were all gone! Great fear seized their hearts.

"Then, there was a scream down the hall, from another nurse. One of her patients, who was in a cast and could not have possibly gotten off the bed, was gone and the cast was left behind. It would have taken doctors a couple of hours to have removed it. The nurse had gone to get the patient some ice, and when she returned, he disappeared right before her eyes just as she entered the door. It was incredible!

"Other nurses discovered that some of their patients were gone, too. It was such a shock, even under their nerves trained for emergencies, that they became hysterical.

"One of the patients had his radio on when the news flash came over the radio about the terrible tragedy of thousands of people disappearing, and he began screaming as loud as he could. He had been saved once and knew the teaching of the second coming of the Lord, so he knew right off what had happened.

"He made so much noise that all the nurses on the second floor rushed to his room, and he told them that the Lord had come because it had just come over the radio. Some of the nurses fainted, and some became hysterical and were not able to control themselves.

"When Hazel heard that the Lord had come and caught people away, it was too much for her mind. Oh, Hester," Mrs. Pickett wailed, "it's so terrible my Hazel has gone insane. They called me from the hospital, and they have had to put her in a strait jacket. I just can't bear it! She was so intelligent.

"I don't know about all those people disappearing. I haven't had time to think much about it. Do you really think, Hester, that the Lord has come?" She looked as if she was waiting for a sentence of death.

"Yes, it is true, Mrs. Pickett. The Lord has caught His people away."

Hester told her about Nancy and her going to

church the night before, and about Nancy's finding the Lord; also, how she had discovered Nancy and Mother Collins being gone and what she had found in Mother Collins' bedroom.

To Mrs. Pickett, it seemed fantastic, because she had never been one to believe that the Lord was really coming for His people. She did not want to believe it now, so she tried to make herself believe that it was not true. What she really wanted Hester to say was that it was not true, but she emphatically stated the fact without hesitance.

"The Lord would not bring all this sorrow upon mankind. He is a just God and He is too honorable to do such a thing. Why should He come and steal people away from the earth?"

"The Lord Jesus has not stolen anyone from the earth. He came for what was rightfully His. You know we could have been ready, Mrs. Pickett. You knew the teaching of His second coming, didn't you?" she asked accusingly.

"I have heard about it all my life, but I did not really think it could be so. I have not heard it preached in a long time, because I have not been to church in years. I have had too many other things to do. I have my own work through the week, and then we usually go fishing on Sunday or do something else that is a lot more enjoyable than going to church. My husband never cared much for church. His theory has always been: 'What is to be will be and we have no control over it.' "

"That is not true. The Lord gave every one of us his own free choice to get ready and go with Him. Through His blood, all mankind could have been ready this morning. By rejecting His blood, we have been left behind."

"I do not believe it," Mrs. Pickett interrupted. "It just cannot be true. I refuse to believe such an idle tale."

That remark stirred Hester's indignation.

"Well, believe what you will, Mrs. Pickett. People like you are the cause of many of us being left behind. You are just too stubborn to believe God's Word."

By this time, Hester was boiling with anger on the inside. All the pity she had felt for Mrs. Pickett when she found her crying was gone.

Looking Mrs. Pickett straight in the face with accusing eyes, she said, "You are the cause of your daughter's being insane. If you had taught her the right way, she might have been caught away with the Lord."

Tears were rolling down Hester's cheeks; and she was thinking if her mother had taken her to church and taught her the right way, she might not have been left behind either; but she had had no encouragement.

"Mothers like you have a lot to think about this morning," she cried.

With this, she turned on her heels and rushed madly away as if Mrs. Pickett were a poisonous viper.

That last remark wounded Mrs. Pickett's dignity. She opened her mouth to give Hester a good tongue lashing, but before she had time to say one word Hester was racing down the street. She looked after her with cold fear gripping her heart.

Mrs. Pickett tried hard not to believe that the Lord had come and that that was really where all those people were. She had accepted the fact when Hester came up, but she had tried to steel her heart against it before she left.

"I refuse to believe that nonsense! What is to be will be," she muttered, "and we have nothing to do with it."

Deep down in her heart she knew that what Hester had said was true. She had not been the right kind of mother to her daughter, but she would not admit it.

There were many affecting and touching scenes for Hester to witness that were a result of the coming of the Lord. No one individual could witness all of them nor describe the horrors. Every way one turned was evidence that the rapture had really taken place. If there was only some hope that one could get ready and make the rapture yet, but all hope was gone. Hester was in the Tribulation Period with thousands of others. It just did not seem real, but she knew by now that it could not be a dream.

Yesterday, when she heard the message about the coming of the Lord and the Tribulation, it seemed so far in the future, but now it was over. If she could have looked into the morrow, things would have been different, but that is the way of life—today belongs to man, tomorrow belongs to God. Only God had known what the morrow would bring. Warning had been given for people to get ready, and He had told them that His Son would come at an unexpected time.

A large crowd was gathered in front of the Epworth Funeral Home. What would a crowd be interested in at a funeral home on a morning like this?

Wesley Bertram, the undertaker, was saying excitedly: "I tell you, I just don't know! In all the years that I have been in business, nothing like this has ever happened before. I have looked and looked, but I cannot find it. I have done all that I can do. I have called and called the police, but the line has been busy, and I cannot get them."

Hester pushed forward in the crowd until she could see to whom the words were being addressed. A well-dressed man in a grey suit and hat, with a large diamond ring that sparkled in the sunlight as he moved his left hand, stood directly in front of Wesley Bertram.

"I think this is the limit. It is absurd to think that last night you brought the body of my wife here to prepare it for burial, and now, this morning, you tell me it is gone.

"Now, if you think just because John Dresden is a man of wealth, and you can pull a stunt like this and get me to give a reward for the return of her body and you get an enormous sum out of me, you have another thought coming! I will sue you! That is what

I will do! I will sue you for every penny you have! I will give you until twelve o'clock noon, and if the body is not here at that time, I have no more to say. I will let my lawyer do the rest. Remember, old man, with the influence that I have, you will not be able ever to build up another business."

Wesley Bertram shook his head helplessly as he was at his wits end. What was there left for him to do? For hours he had searched for the missing body, and he had not been able to figure out a solution to the perplexing problem. Unless someone had stolen the body because they knew this man was a man of wealth, there was no other way out. That must be it, because surely no one would play a prank like that—but who would do such a thing? All the years he had been in business, he had never heard of anyone's stealing a body, so it never entered his mind that he should leave someone to guard the body.

The man with the big diamond on his finger started to turn away, and Hester clutched at his sleeve.

"Sir," she said.

John Dresden whirled and looked down into her face. Her big, black eyes looked like pools of torture. Because he was very much annoyed, he started to speak roughly to her. He was used to having his way, and his previous conversation had upset him very much. Storming and threatening the undertaker did not seem to help matters any, because he still stubbornly contended that he did not know what to do.

"What is it?" he managed to say kindly.

"Was your wife a Christian?"

"Why, come to think of it, she was," he said, stroking his chin with his left hand. "She was always talking religion, but I never paid her much mind. I let her do whatever would make her happy. I had my work, and she had plenty of time to do anything she wanted to.

"But say, young lady, what would the disappearing of my wife's body have to do with her being a Christian?"

John Dresden was surprised at himself for taking up so much time with this young lady. Any other time, he would have brushed her aside and gone on his way without giving her a second thought.

The excited crowd moved in a little closer to hear what Hester was saying to John Dresden. Maybe she had some valuable information that would help solve this great mystery of the missing body.

"If she was a true child of God, she had the 'blessed hope.'"

"What do you mean, girl? Don't talk in riddles. I am anxious for this mystery to be cleared. If you are able to help us, speak at once."

Hester spoke very low, but every one in the crowd could hear the words she was saying.

"The Lord came for His own around six o'clock this morning. Since your wife was a Christian, her body was changed and caught up to be reunited with the soul the same as those that were in the ground. The resurrection of the saints of God took place this morning when those many thousands disappeared from the earth."

Awe-stricken John Dresden stared in unbelief.

"If you will go to the graveyard, I am sure you will find that many of the graves have been disturbed."

John Dresden and the crowd rushed away going to the cemeteries, and Hester stood alone gazing after them.

A few moments later, she decided she would follow them and see the results of the resurrection for herself. Before she arrived, she heard the cries of the people, and she knew they were witnessing the unbelievable results of the resurrection.

Before an open grave, about twenty feet from the gate, stood the well-dressed man she had talked to at the funeral home, with a handkerchief in his hand, crying and looking down into the open grave. For a moment she stood by his side, but he did not seem to notice her.

The scripture, I Corinthians 15:42-44, came to Hester's mind. "So also is the resurrection of the dead. It is sown in corruption; it is raised in incorruption:

"It is sown in dishonour; it is raised in glory: it is sown in weakness; it is raised in power:

"It is sown a natural body; it is raised a spiritual body. There is a natural body, and there is a spiritual body."

"It is terrible, isn't it?" John said tremulously.

"Yes, it is," she answered. "Now you understand

what I was telling you about the disappearing of your wife's body, don't you?"

"Yes," he answered with a choked voice, "I understand now. It is so hard to have to face it, though."

His face revealed deep suffering, and the muscles in his face twitched. The agony he felt was almost more than he could bear.

Hester hastily made her way through the cemetery, pausing only a few seconds here and there before an open grave.

Widow Blandon lived five blocks from the cemetery, and when Hester passed, all was quiet. Two years ago when her husband was killed in an automobile accident, she was left with five small children. The road of life had been rugged, and she worried from one day to the next about what she would do on tomorrow for food, but the Lord always provided.

Sunday night, the load was so heavy. There was no bread for them to eat, the purse was empty, and the baby was sick. Finally, after getting the sick child to sleep, she cried and prayed until after midnight, and then fell into a deep sleep. God's tomorrow could not be seen, and she did not know that in a few hours her troubles would all be over.

At ten minutes before six, the alarm went off, and she dragged her weary body out of bed. Every muscle in her body was tired and strained, and it seemed she had no more than closed her eyes before it was time to get up. The burden upon her heart was almost more than she could bear, but she must try to find a few hours work to get something for the children to eat.

All of a sudden, the room was lighted up with the glory of God. She, too, heard the cry: "Behold, the bridegroom cometh; go ye out to meet Him." Something like liquid fire poured over her body. The change had come. She was changed in a moment, in the twinkling of an eye, and her little ones that slept were caught up with her. The glorious morn had come!

Linda Jordan lived two doors down from Widow Blandon. Linda had been saved for a number of years, but she had received many cruel tortures from her husband who tried to make her backslide. Sometimes he tried to make her blaspheme the name of her Lord by holding her and twisting her arm until it was almost unbearable. He tried her in every way he could think of, but she always came out victorious. He would even tell lies on her to the pastor and the members of her church; but they did not believe them, because they knew the kind of man he was and the great persecutions she received from him.

He was standing by her bed when the rapture took place. She had been to the revival the night before, and he was always angry when a revival was in progress. A little before six, he called her. With many oaths he told her to get up and cook his breakfast.

Sleepily, she raised up and looked at the clock. Was it possible that she had overslept?

"Why, honey, it is an hour before it will be time

for me to fix your breakfast. You must have looked at the clock wrong."

With this he went into a rage.

"Don't talk back to me. You go out and stay every night at that disgraceful church of yours, then you don't want to get up and cook my breakfast. That religion has ruined our home. At this rate our marriage will soon be in a divorce court." His face darkened with rage.

Linda was dumbfounded and stared with surprise. He had done many unheard of things, but this was the first time he had tried a thing like this.

"Don't just sit there like an idiot! I mean get up! I want you to stop going to that old church. I forbid you to go any more! If you have to go to a church, why don't you act sensible about it and go to one that is respected by the better class of people in this town? I am ashamed of you!

"All you can hear in the pool room and everywhere you go is what that preacher down there is preaching. Some of the men have heard just about enough of it."

Tears filled her eyes, and he scornfully said, "You don't need to cry and think you can get my sympathy. Get up!" he said with a curse. "Maybe if you get up an hour or so earlier, you won't be so anxious to go to church every night."

All of a sudden, a bright light illuminated the room. One moment Jordan's wife was there, and the next moment she was gone. She, too, heard the cry, "Behold, the bridegroom cometh; go ye out to meet Him." She was changed in a moment, in the twinkling of an eye, and was caught up to be with her Lord forever! The glorious morn had come!

Henry Jordan could not believe his eyes. It was incredible! His wife had vanished into thin air.

An oath was about to escape his lips, but great fear seized his heart and checked him. He did not know what to make of it. He looked all around, but he could not find any trace of her. Madly he rushed from the house, screaming and pulling his hair.

Hester heard a shrill scream pierce the air as she walked slowly down the street. It was the most blood curdling sound she had ever heard, and she almost froze in her tracks. Again the scream reached her ears, and the door of a small yellow house down the street was thrown open.

Betty Wren, with disheveled hair, eyes wide with terror, pale as death, and gasping for breath, stood clinging to the side of the door screaming: "Help! Help!"

Betty Wren was the sister of Bob Wren, and Bob was the husband of a quiet mere wisp of a girl, and the father of two children. Through the channel of gossip, Hester knew the history of their family.

Bob had never settled down, and, to tell the truth, he had just been a good for nothing all his life. He would not work half the time, and the neighbors said he was just a shiftless no good. He would leave his wife and children alone all hours of the night while he ran around drinking and flirting with other women.

Hester was not acquainted with his wife, but she had heard many good things about her. She was a good Christian girl and a wonderful, precious mother to her children. According to reports from the neighbors, she really had a hard time. Not only did she have to keep house, wash and care for the children, but she had to work at public work to help support the children and herself. What a cruel fate had befallen such a wonderful girl who would have made some boy a devoted wife.

All this and more was rushing swiftly through Hester's mind as she made her way across the street and up the walk to Betty. Betty was so excited she lost her power of speech, so she seized Hester wildly by the arm and almost dragged her into the house. An unexpected scream escaped Hester's lips as Betty Wren pulled her through the door into the bedroom and pointed to the horrible tragedy. Hester thought she was prepared for anything, but the scene she saw in Bob Wren's bedroom was one she felt she could never erase from her mind. Her eyes focused on one thing, and that was the body of Bob Wren dangling from the ceiling. His eyes were popping from their sockets, and his tongue lolled out with blood running out the corners of his mouth. He was dead!

Hester looked with dismay and unbelief at what her eyes revealed. The unfaithful, drunkard husband of a Christian wife had committed suicide!

Betty moved closer to him and made a desperate attempt to pull him down, but it was all in vain. She was beside herself and did not realize what she was doing.

Hester spoke to her in a commanding tone. "Betty, it is too late. Don't do that. It won't help matters."

Hester's commanding voice brought her out of her stupor, and she turned a haggard face with drooping eyes toward her.

"But, he can't be dead! Please tell me my brother is not dead!"

Hester took her by the shoulders and pushed her toward the door. After trying to make her comfortable in a big armchair in the parlor, she slowly and softly closed the door to the death room.

With a desperate attempt, Betty tried to talk, but for a moment it was just a groan from a distressed heart.

Her face shadowed as she finally managed to say, "I don't know what made him do it."

Suddenly, she sat up straight in her chair and sighed deeply, drawing in her breath.

Where was her sister-in-law and the children? Had Jenny left him? Was that the cause? Had he come home and found a note telling him she was through?

She stood to her feet with deep-seated determination written on her countenance as if she felt Hester would try to stop her from doing what she was about to do. Rushing toward the closed door, she turned the knob and entered the room.

With troubled eyes she looked at the beds. Yes, they had been slept in. If Jenny had left, it would have had to have been after she went to bed last night. As she scrutinized every nook and corner trying to find a note, she dared not get close enough to the body to touch it nor would she look at it.

There was no note to be found, but her bewildering eyes fell upon a newspaper lying on the floor. With a trembling hand, she stooped to pick it up. She took in the headlines at once: THOUSANDS OF PEOPLE MYSTERIOUSLY DISAPPEARED! Blinking her eyes, she reread it; but she did not understand what it meant. Then, for the first time, Hester realized that Betty did not know that the Lord had come. Where had she been all the morning,

She was as pale as death as she walked over to Hester and showed her the paper to see if she knew what it was all about. It was beyond her.

With quivering lips she asked, "Do you know what this means?"

"Yes," Hester softly answered. "The Lord came this morning and took everybody away that was saved."

Betty listened breathlessly. Her fists clenched and unclenched as she stood staring incredulously at Hester.

"It just can't be possible! It just can't be! I heard that would happen some day, but I never gave it much thought. In fact," she paused in deep thought, "Jenny often spoke of the coming of the Lord. I thought Jenny always looked her prettiest when she talked about Him. That was all she seemed to be really living for. It was absurd to me, but I never told her so because it was such a beautiful thought to her.

"Although Bob is my brother and he is d-e-a-d," she stammered, blinking back the tears, "he never gave her too much happiness. He caused her so much heartache, but she took it better than anyone I have ever seen. I told her many times if I were her I would leave and never let Bob know where I had gone, but she kept praying and expecting her God to deliver her. Now, God has delivered her, but not in the way Jenny prayed.

"I wonder where she is? It is strange that she isn't home. She seldom ever went anywhere. This is going to be a terrible shock to her."

Hester gave her a bewildered look and said: "Betty, isn't it clear in your mind yet what has happened? Jenny is gone! She has been carried away to be with her Lord forever."

Betty looked as if she was going to faint as the real truth dawned upon her.

"It just can't be! Poor little Jenny's not gone!" she exclaimed, flinging herself into Hester's arms. Then, she raised her head from Hester's shoulder and looking into her eyes she said: "Now it is all plain. I mean Bob's death. He must have awakened, missed Jenny and the children, and gone to search for them. When he found this paper, he realized that what Jenny had warned him about so many times had really taken place. Poor Bob," she sighed.

Betty was still talking as Hester made a hasty exit. She had forgotten that she had started to go to see some of her mother's friends and see if they knew that the Lord had really come. She knew without a doubt that they had been left behind.

Hester tried to shut out the horrible scene of Bob dangling at the end of a rope from the top of the ceiling, but it was impossible. In hell he lifted up his eyes, and now he was in worse trouble If he had been living for the Lord, this would have never happened.

At last, Hester approached a large apartment house almost hid by shrubbery and trees, sitting back from the road. She did not wait for the elevator boy, but she took the steps two at a time, and soon she was standing at the door of Martha and Wilma's apartment on the second floor. She rapped loudly on the door and waited impatiently, shifting from one foot to the other.

"Why doesn't someone answer?"

Just as she started to knock again, Wilma cautiously cracked the door and peered into the dimly lighted hall.

Hester stared with astonishment. It was a different looking Wilma to what she had always seen. Her hair had not been combed, her lips were purple, her eyes red-rimmed from crying, and her troubled eyes looked as if they had sunken ever so far in her head. Between nervous fingers, she carried a half smoked cigarette.

When Wilma saw Hester, she gave a sigh of relief and threw the door wide open.

"Come in, Hester," she tremulously said.

Hester took in the room at a glance, and her piercing eyes rested upon a late edition of the paper lying on the hassock. She was convinced that Wilma knew that the Lord had come.

Hester sat down. Stony silence prevailed.

Wilma casually asked, "What is your mother doing today?"

It was strange to hear someone speak casually when so much had happened.

Hester started to speak, but Wilma interrupted. "Oh, you need not answer my question. What is the need of our acting like this? I know what has happened. The Lord has come! Why don't you say it? You just as well say it as to sit there and look like that," she bitterly said.

"I wish I were dead! I loathe this day! I never thought I would ever live to see a day like this. It is enough to drive me mad! I feel so sorry for Martha. She has been almost hysterical."

"Where is Martha?" Hester asked, looking through the open door into the next room.

"I don't know," she replied. "The poor kid rushed out of the house when she heard about it, and I have been so worried about her. I am afraid something has happened to her. She was wild with fear!

"Why God would do us like this is more than I can understand. It is terrible the way people are troubled today. I had planned for a big day and now it is ruined. All because. . . ."

Hester stood to her feet suddenly and interrupted Wilma.

"Don't say it!" she shouted. "You talk as if you blame God for all of this! It is not God that you should blame. You should blame yourself! You could have been ready. After all, God went to a lot of trouble that mankind could escape this horrible thing. Think of the many thousands that took the passage of escape that was offered them through Calvary. You know Jesus died for you as well as He did for those people who were caught away!"

"Who said they wanted to be caught away?" Wilma sneered with quivering lips. "Don't you dare talk to me in that tone of voice! If I want to be preached to, I will go to church! It is none of your business, but my own, if I did not accept the Lord. Now, is it?" she demanded scornfully. Her fiery, piercing eyes flashed like a viper that was ready to strike.

Wilma was a shrewd woman, and Hester had always resented her being a special friend of her mother, but her mother always thought Wilma was such a good sport.

With a meek up-lifted profile, Hester apologized. "Wilma, I am sorry. I did not mean to preach or be abrupt. I am sure every one has free choice to do as he wants to do in this old world. We can accept the Lord or reject Him.

"If we reject Him, we will have to take the conse-

quences," she added under her breath, because she
knew it would not do for Wilma to hear her last
remark.

Wilma was very discomposed and would not be
quieted until she had said many ruthless things about
God and His work. Hester's pulse quickened, and her
cheeks flushed a deep pink as this woman of the world
irreverently spoke of the Lord to whom Hester paid
honorable tribute with the highest degree of respect.

"You are the dumbest person I have ever seen,
Hester. What do you mean upholding a God who has
left you in a predicament like this?"

Hester's hands were cold and clenched, and her
heart pounded madly in her bosom; but she did not
attempt to say more to Wilma. When Wilma went
into the next room to answer the telephone, Hester
crept softly from the apartment like a wounded animal.

When she approached the street again, the scenes
of tragedy still prevailed as a result of the coming
of the Lord.

"My God!" she groaned, "this horror of being left
behind!"

CHAPTER VIII

Jim lived through the days immediately following the rapture with great agony. The days were long, but the nights were longer. The awful catastrophe that he found himself in was almost more than his mind could comprehend. He felt, at times, that he would surely wake up from this nightmare and find it to be just another dream, but on the other hand he knew without a shadow of a doubt that it was true.

The remorse he felt was indescribable, but he realized it was too late for regrets. They would not help now. If only he had heeded the many warnings given by his precious mother. She had seen this day through the reading of God's Word and had gotten ready to escape. If he had only known that it would happen in his day, he would have gotten ready. Why didn't he take the Bible and believe it? There was a passage of escape, but now it was closed. He was in the Tribulation Period.

Jim often visited Mother Collins' little bungalow. He walked from room to room and tried to imagine that his mother was still there. He could see her head of silvery locks bent over reading the great Book and praying. He could hear her in the kitchen singing a blessed old hymn with the fervor of a youngster just as she used to do when he was a child.

Then, suddenly, he would be brought back to realization that this would never be. She was gone! She would never pray for him again. Pray! My God, what would he do now with no mother to pray for him? How could he go on living? Sobbingly, he would rush from the house not caring, for the moment, where he was going. If only he could drop into a pool of forgetfulness never to remember or be remembered any more, but Jim had to go on living.

When he was home, life was almost unbearable, because Lucille had not been well a day since Baby Sue disappeared. She would cry over and over, hour after hour, "I want my baby! I want my baby! Jim," she would cry with a voice prompted by a mother's tortured heart, "please bring her to me. Can't you find her anywhere? I can't go on living like this."

Months passed, and Jim watched the change of world events with great anxiety. Mother's Bible was more like her than anything else, so he took it home with him and read and reread the Book of Daniel and Revelation. It used to seem so complicated and far-fetched, but it was all clear to him now. Living in a nation of peace and prosperity, one could not easily conceive all the things prophesied in these books coming to pass.

It was amazing how things had changed. The Man of Sin had brought peace to the whole earth. The distressed nations, with war clouds hanging low and nations actually at war, were anxious to accept a man of his ability and profound knowledge. In the eyes of many, he was just the man that the world had needed for a long time. Jim knew it was a temporary sham peace and that it would not last, because in the Book of Daniel he had read that by peace he would destroy many.

The perplexities of the nations were solved. Problems that great statesmen had tried to solve for years but had found no solution, were now solved in a few moments by this great superman that had dropped down from heaven and said he was the very Son of God. Should anyone doubt he could produce evidence that he was the Son of God? The Jews were ready to die for him. They had looked for their Redeemer for many years, and now he had come.

No one dared criticize him on the street, because anything might happen to them if they did. Houses were being burned nightly, and people were disappearing from the face of the earth, without loved ones ever knowing their fate, just because they had dared voice their opinion in public that this man could not be the Son of God.

The Jews were the happiest people in the world. Their temple was rebuilt, and they worshiped in it and offered their sacrifices as in days of old. They were in the height of their glory. This great man of power favored the Jews above all peoples of the earth. He did not want anything for himself, but he divided the spoil among the people. Why should he want anything? He was the son of God.

In a few months, many people forgot that there had been a rapture—but not Jim. The gnawing, aching pain was ever with him to remind him what a fool he had been to reject the Christ of Calvary.

Lucille awoke late one morning and said, "Honey, call Doctor Wilson. I am having another sinking spell. I don't feel like I can live much longer if I don't get a doctor at once."

Jim sighed deeply, and with a heavy heart he hurried to the telephone. He just could not lose Lucille, because she was all he had left. What would life be like if she should die?

With shaking hands, he picked up the receiver and dialed Doctor Wilson. The ringing of the telephone continued for six, long rings, and just as Jim was about to give up in despair, the receiver was lifted from its cradle at the other end of the line, and a gruff voice said, "Hello."

"Is this Doctor Wilson's office?" Jim asked in a business like tone.

"This is he speaking," the coarse voice answered.

For a moment Jim was startled, but he managed to collect his wits and say, "Doctor, you must have a terrible cold. You don't sound natural. What has happened to you?"

"Nothing has happened to me," he replied with a stern voice. "I feel better than I ever felt in my life. The way the day has started off, I would not be surprised that it will be the greatest day of my life."

"Listen, Doctor, I want you to come at once. Lucille is having another bad spell. Will you please hurry?"

The doctor bluntly asked, "Jim, do you have the mark?"

With that question, Jim almost dropped the receiver. The mark! My God! The Mark of the Beast? His heart was pounding madly in his bosom, his tongue felt an inch thick, and his lips were numb.

There was silence for the space of a minute, and then the doctor asked, "Jim, are you there?"

"Yes, I am here," Jim managed to murmur weakly.

"Well, speak up, my boy. Do you have the mark of security?"

"Doctor, you don't mean the Mark of the Beast?" Jim asked breathlessly.

Time seemed to stand still, and the clock on the mantel ticked loudly. Would it drown out the doctor's voice?

"Yes, some might call it that."

"No, Doctor Wilson!" Jim cried. "Don't you take that mark! It is the mark of doom! If you take that mark, you can never get right with God. You will be like a demon from hell."

"What do you mean, Jim, talking that way?" the doctor sternly interrupted. "Don't you realize it is dangerous for you to have such talk? It is blasphemy. I could have you put to death for making remarks like that, so let this be a warning to you. Of course, I have the mark that you think is so terrible," he proudly answered.

"Didn't you see the evening paper or hear the reports over the radio that everything would be frozen after twelve o'clock last night? You cannot buy or sell unless you have this mark. I could not open my office this morning unless I took the mark first. My nurse cannot assist me until she takes the mark. She has gone now to take it.

"Don't be foolish, Jim. I have always considered you a sensible type of boy. You know, fellow, I would not advise you wrong. I have known you all your life. I was there and helped bring you into the world. Have I ever advised you wrong?

"It is the greatest tonic I have ever found for nerve trouble. I don't feel jittery at all as I usually do this time of morning.

"It is like the war days now. We used the rationing book then, but now it is the Mark of the Beast. It is less complicated this way. There is not a thing to be alarmed about. Of course, there will be some that will get hysterical over the matter for a while, but they will get over it. You cannot draw your money out of the bank without this mark or get groceries from your grocery man. You know you cannot hold out against all of this. This is the most popular thing of the day, and you do not want to be behind the times. Why, you will not be considered anything with the people that really count if you do not take the mark.

"They are setting up offices throughout the city. I saw one two blocks from your house as I came down town this morning.

"I will be glad to come if you will take the mark;

but it would cause my license to be revoked, and I might even lose my life if I should come without your taking the mark. We have been given strict orders to minister to no one who does not have the mark. This is the situation as it stands at the moment.

"Don't be stupid. If you and Lucille will both take the mark, then give me a ring and I will be on my way. You know you love your wife enough to do a simple thing as this to get her medical aid."

With a ruthless good-by, Doctor Wilson slammed down the receiver, and Jim stood before the telephone in a daze. Did he hear correctly? Had the doctor really said those scornful things? His fists clenched and unclenched, and he sighed taking a deep breath. The flaming truth of the works of the devil had just come over the line. What could he do? How could he manage to get medical aid for Lucille without taking the mark? He must find a way. Surely there was a way if he could find it.

The conversation left Jim discomposed, and he forgot he must hurry back to the sick room of his suffering wife. He felt so deplorable. If only he had gotten right with the Lord before it was too late he would not have to be going through all this. Suddenly, he was brought to his senses by a piercing cry from Lucille's room. He hurried to the bedside of his wife who was in great agony. Cold beads of perspiration had popped out on her forehead, and her lips were turning purple. She was striving to keep back the groans, but to no avail. At once, Jim knew if he was going to do anything for her, he would have to do it quickly. If only he had time to reason this thing out. His brain felt numb and his mind refused to function.

"My God! Won't you have mercy upon me?" he choked.

The tears gathered in his eyes and he tried to pray just as he had tried many other times since God's people had been taken out, but he could not pray. The demon power of darkness had him surrounded, and he was as one being mocked as he tried to pray.

The earth had been turned into the hands of the devil. He had been told this time would come, but like many others, he had never considered it seriously.

"Jim," Lucille said in a low tone, "is the doctor coming?"

Jim's heart beat faster. How could he tell her, and how would she take the shock? She was so helpless and pathetic.

Jim could not help crying as he answered, "No, he is not coming."

"What do you mean he is not coming? Wasn't he there?" she cried.

"Yes,—he was—there," Jim drawled, "but, honey, things have changed overnight. People have to have something besides money now to get medical aid."

That kind of uncouth talk was all a puzzle to Lucille, and Jim could see she did not understand.

"You remember, during the war days certain

things were frozen like canned goods, meats, sugar, tires, automobiles, building materials and various other items? Well, honey, now you do not have to have a rationing book, but you have to have the Mark of the Beast."

Jim winced as if he had been given a great blow as he said those words, but Lucille did not seem dumbfounded at all.

Tortured eyes were turned upon Jim with a pleading look of a small helpless child.

"Don't we have the money to take it, Jim? We have saved for a rainy day. Remember? Jim, I need medical aid as I have never needed it before."

Two big tears rolled down her cheeks and splashed on the white sheet.

"I must have a doctor," she said earnestly.

Jim stood in deep thought. This could not be real. This could not be he, Jim Collins, who had had a Christian mother and had been taught the ways of the Lord. Ministers tried to describe what a time of horror it would be, but no one had ever been able to give a taste of what it would really be like when it was actually faced.

"No, honey, it does not cost money," he said in a faltering tone. "It is free!"

Free? The doctor had said it was free, but how free is it? All it costs you is your soul.

Jim bent a little closer to her and said, "Listen, honey, you have to sell your soul to take this mark. We will never see our baby or mother again. We would have to give up all chances of finding God and being delivered from this world of hatred and turmoil."

He thought surely this would help her to realize the seriousness of taking the mark, but Lucille did not understand. Her body was racked by continuous, hot, piercing pains which shot through her weak body; and her body was crying to be delivered from the awful pain.

"Honey, I would gladly give all we have saved to get you medical aid, but we cannot sell our soul and become like a demon from hell. Oh, darling, we have suffered so much and if we take this mark, all hope will be gone forever. We will never be happy again. Think how lonely we have been without little Sue and mother. The price is too great. We cannot afford to pay it. I feel sure, there will be some way if we will just wait a while and think things through."

"Jim," she said in a low tone, "haven't I been a good wife to you? Wasn't I a good mother to your baby? Jim, if this were you," she pleaded, "I would gladly do anything for you. Don't you believe that, Jim?"

She raised herself on her elbow and sat up in bed. Her black hair glistened in the dim light. A curl fell down over one eye; and she looked so weak and helpless. How could he refuse her? He loved her so much. She had been a good wife. She had not been a Christian wife, but neither had he been a Christian husband. He could not blame her for his being left behind. He should have been the one to lead her.

Maybe he could have saved her from all this heart-ache if he had gotten right with the Lord and lived a devout Christian life before her.

He was trying to make the greatest decision that he had ever had to make in his life. There seemed no other way out but for him to take the mark.

"All right, honey," he said in a tender, trembling voice, "I will be back in a little while. Try to keep your mind off your suffering as much as you can. I will get you medical aid as soon as possible."

Jim bent low and gently kissed her on the brow. A tear rolled down his cheek and fell on her face.

Jim picked up his mother's Bible and began to leaf through it. Every scripture on the second coming of the Lord was marked, and he observed a blot here and there where a tear had fallen from his precious mother's eyes as she read the promises and prayed that Jim would get ready before it was too late.

Time had passed by, and the rapture had taken place just as his mother believed it would, and there he stood left behind and about to sell his soul.

"My God," he prayed, "do come to my rescue. Please, God, do help me."

He hugged his mother's Bible close to him and placed a last good-by kiss upon the soft, black cover. If Mother were there, she would know just what to do. She always knew what to do in hard places.

Finally, he tore himself away from the Bible with its memories of yesterday, picked up his hat, opened the front door and stepped out on the porch. His mind was made up. He would have to take the mark. What a horrible thought to be on your way to sell your soul—not an arm, a leg or eye. If that was all, or if it were both feet, eyes, and hands, it would not be so terrible, but it was your very soul. All Jim's life he had planned to go to heaven some day, but now he was about to determine his destiny forever.

As he slowly walked down the street, in his imagination he could hear his mother praying just as she used to. His heart was filled with remorse, but it was too late to recall those many opportunities he had had to escape this hour that he was now facing.

A man coming toward him drew his attention. As he came nearer, he saw a man with a countenance such as he had never seen on a human being. His eyes were like fiery darts, and he looked Jim straight in the eye. A queer looking mark stood out in his forehead. He was carrying the Mark of the Beast! As the man passed him, he felt the very presence of the devil. He drew in a long, deep breath as he remembered he was on his way to do the same thing that man had done. What an awful feeling to look at someone and know he was doomed and could never get right with the Lord. Jim shuddered, turned and stared after the disappearing figure.

When he passed by Fairview church, he felt an urge to stop in one more time. The building, with the stained-glass windows revealing a warm welcome, reminded him of the Rock of Ages. He reverently pushed the door open and stepped into the main auditorium. Slowly he walked down the aisle—the aisle he had walked down hundreds of times. The endearment of this precious building was greater this morning than ever before.

He paused for a few moments at his mother's sacred pew, and the tears began trickling down his sad, drawn face. How his heart ached for God's people who used to worship there.

Hundreds had wept their way through to victory at that altar, but how many of those people had stood true and were caught away? He knelt at the altar, but he could not feel any spirit of prayer. The powers of darkness were pressing so, he could not put words together to form a prayer.

The depressed feeling for what he was about to do was almost too great. He paused on the threshold of the church door and gave one last lingering look. The tears blinded his vision; then he turned suddenly and ran down the church steps toward the office to sell his soul.

Nick, the operator of Jake's Station, was filling Burt Mill's gas tank. Jim gasped when he saw the Mark of the Beast in Nick's forehead. Burt, he thought, must not have the mark. Why should Burt be getting gas if everything was frozen like the doctor said? Just then, Burt stretched forth his hand to pay for the service rendered, and Jim saw the Mark of the Beast in the palm of his right hand. The gnawing remembrance of his mother and the church rolled over and over in his mind as he walked the rest of the journey to the office

with the large sign in big, bold, black letters—TAKE
THE MARK HERE—hanging over the door. It was a
small, portable, white building.

Jim stood perfectly rigid from head to toe just outside the door for a few minutes. Did he dare turn
and run? That was what he felt like doing. The
Spirit of God was dealing with his heart, but must he
go through with it for Lucille's sake?

The sun was shining from the blue above, and the
birds were singing and jumping from limb to limb, but
all the sunshine, joy and happiness had fled from Jim.

He was trembling all over as he finally gained
enough courage to step through the door into the small
office. The room was simple with a large, dark desk
and a shining instrument on its top. A man with a
fierce countenance sat in a squeaky chair behind the
desk. His eyes were like fiery darts, and his features
were like the Beast. The demon powers of darkness
were so thick, Jim's knees bent, and he almost fell to
the hard floor. Something like invisible hands were
reaching for him. Once, he started to turn and flee;
but then, in his imagination, he could hear Lucille
saying, "Honey, if this were you, you know I would do
anything for you." He had promised her that he would
get her medical aid, and he could not let her down.
How could he go back and break the news to her that
he had decided not to take the mark, and there would
be no doctor?

"No, I cannot do that," he choked under his breath.

"This is the price I will have to pay. There is no alternative."

The man behind the desk looked at Jim with penetrating eyes and said with a sneer: "You have nothing to fear. I was nervous before I took it, but all the fear left me. This is a real tonic for your nerves. I know you tremble because of that old Book called the Bible, but it is nothing but a bunch of rotten superstition. You will find out I am telling you the truth after you have taken the mark. You will never have any more respect for that Book. In fact, you will hate it for the fear it has caused you all your life and kept you from having good times."

"Don't say any more!" Jim cried. "Don't torture me like this! Hurry and get it over with!"

While Jim stood in the little office about to take the Mark of the Beast, the death angel entered Lucille's bedroom.

"I don't want to die!" she cried in terror. "Please, God! don't let me die! I have lived a wicked life. I said I did not believe you existed, but I knew you did all the time. Oh, God, I cannot die like this."

She stared wildly about the room.

"Mother Collins," she shrieked, "please, please come here and pray for me. I am dying. In a few more minutes I will be in eternity without God. I said that I did not believe in your salvation, but I knew it was right because God's Bible teaches it. I wanted to be sophisticated, and that is why I put on a bold front. Please, Mother Collins, forgive me and come pray that my soul may find God."

There was no answer except the echo of her own cries. If it had been possible, Mother Collins would have gladly come to Lucille's rescue, but she had waited too late to cry for help. Mother Collins was gone to be with the Lord forever.

Again she screamed, "Someone help me! The demons of hell are here to usher my soul into that terrible place called hell! I'm lost!" she shrieked. "I feel the flames of hell! I'm lost!" Then she started to shout it again, but the words choked in her throat, and her soul lifted up its eyes in hell to suffer the pangs of torment forever.

The only sign of life in the room was a breeze gently blowing the curtains in and out. The body lay motionless.

At that moment, Jim stood before the man with the devilish looking countenance and a shining instrument in his hand. If Jim had only known that Lucille was dead, he might have run from the room, but it was too late now.

He stretched forth his right hand and said, "I am ready."

Looking Jim straight in the eye he asked, "Why don't you take it in the forehead where it will be easily seen? That will help entice others to take it."

Jim gritted his teeth and replied: "Go on, I tell you, and get it over with! I don't want it in my forehead. It is not a mark to be proud of! I am taking it because I have to," he said sobbingly. "I had the dearest Christian mother a boy ever had." With quivering lips he went on saying, "She told me about this time and warned me to get ready to meet the Lord. I know you are making light of this, but it is true anyway. I am not in darkness. I know the Lord came, and God's people were caught away. Look at me as if you think I have lost my mind, but I know what I say is the truth. Now! hurry and give me the mark so I can get a doctor for my wife!"

Two big tears rolled down his pale cheeks from under his closed eyelids. He was selling his soul. Mother Collins' prayers would never be answered, and the Lord's death was in vain for him.

The man raised the shining instrument, then it descended toward Jim's hand. Closer and closer it came, then it touched the palm of his hand. It felt colder than any ice Jim had ever felt. Something shot up his arm and traveled on to his heart. It was amazing how his countenance suddenly changed. Like magic he had been turned into a different man. His eyes glittered, and his lips curled into a sneer. Jim had never been one to swear, but now the blasphemies began to roll from his lips as a great torrent. What a great change had come over him.

After telling the man to send someone to 305 North Main Street to give his wife the mark, he dashed out of the door into the sunlight like a mad man. He looked up into the heavens and dared God, if there be such a being, to come down. He called God every rotten, filthy name he could think of—there were many since he had sold himself wholly to the devil. He was an instrument in the hands of the devil to be used as he used the demons of hell. His heart was filled with hatred for the Bible and God's people.

"What an old-fogyish mother I had," he murmured as he strolled up the street, "to teach me such hellish rot and try to make me think there was one who died for my sins and would save my soul. Of all the nonsense, that was the limit. Now, she has stooped so low as to hide herself away somewhere with all those others and try to convince the world that their Lord has come and caught them away. Why, there has no such thing happened! It is just a bunch of lies! That is what it is!

"She brought me up in a cloud of superstition," he said bitterly, "but now I am free. I'm free!" he shouted.

He threw his head back and gave a hideous laugh.

"I'm glad that freedom has come to me at last. I don't fear that horrible Book any longer. Think how I used to fear it. . . ."

A great love had been born in his heart for the Man of Sin. He had hated him with every ounce of his strength, but now he loved and worshiped him. The doctor had said it was a real tonic and so had the man at the office.

"Yes, they were right!" Jim exclaimed. "I feel calmer than I have felt in many, many days. This mark probably will cure Lucille."

He kept looking at the mark in his hand and admiring it.

"I wish I had let him put it in my forehead," he said aloud as he walked on up the street. "Everybody could see it then."

The spark of hope and love for mankind was missing from Jim's eyes. He passed many people on their way to take the mark, and he could pick out each one that had made up his mind to take the mark. Everyone he passed who had rebellion in his heart against the Beast and the mark made hatred fume within him, and he desired to put him to death. He did not think he was worthy to live if he would not accept the true and only god, his god, the Beast.

Finally, Jim reached home with a heart filled with bitterness toward all of God's people and those who paid tribute to the Lord. He opened the front door with a rough kick, and as he entered the living room, the first thing his eyes fell upon was his mother's Bible. This brought another flood of blasphemies from his lips. He glared at the Bible, and trembling with hatred, he snatched it up and threw it into the fireplace.

With a smirk of satisfaction on his lips, he quickly went to Lucille's bedroom. All was quiet. He paused for a moment, then he called, "Lucille," with a husky voice.

Not realizing that she was dead, he gently shook her.

"Honey, you are going to be all right. I am glad

you insisted on my taking the mark. It is the most wonderful experience I have ever had in my whole life. I feel like a new man. Your worries will soon be over," he said with a loving tone. "I don't imagine Doctor Wilson will have to come after you take the mark, because this is the best tonic you will have ever taken."

Then, he noticed how cold she felt and bent a little closer to her.

"Lucille," he cried. "Lucille!" but there was no answer. "You cannot leave me now since I have found something to make you well."

In his desperation and grief, he shook her roughly, but there was no response.

"She is dead!" he said aloud with a voice of bitterness that would have made any normal person tremble.

Looking up toward the ceiling, as if he were looking in the face of God, and shaking his fist and swearing violently, he said, "You did this! You call yourself God, but you are not the God of the universe! There is only one God and I have found him! We will conquer you," he said positively. "You have caused mankind to suffer! You have deceived many and made people pay tribute to you! At last, the true God has moved upon the scene and has unveiled you before the world. You are being stripped of all your honor and glory! Do you understand!" he shouted.

Throwing himself back in a chair he continued cursing God until the door bell rang. He walked eagerly to the door, and there stood Sam Fergus with the Mark of the Beast in his forehead and a shining instrument clutched in his hand to give Lucille the mark.

"It is too late," Jim said regrettably. "She is dead."

The man asked gruffly, "Where is the body?"

Jim motioned toward the bedroom and went to the telephone to call the funeral home and tell them to come pick up the body. To Jim's surprise, the funeral director wanted to know if the body had the mark on it.

"No, it does not have," Jim answered. "Mr. Fergus who was going to give her the mark is here now, but he arrived too late. I do wish she could have lived long enough to have had the glorious experience of taking the mark."

"I am not allowed to pick up the body and give it a decent burial unless it has the mark on it. I have been notified that bodies without the mark will be picked up in trucks and buried like dogs. If you ask me, that is plenty good enough for them if they refuse to take the mark of our god. You say you are her husband, and you are sure she wanted the mark?"

"That's right," Jim answered sternly. He was a little annoyed at the man for being so cautious.

"Well, in that case, if you will have the mark of our god placed on the body, I will come and pick it up."

Just then, Sam Fergus, with eyes that glittered with demon power like Jim's, stepped through the door which led to the room where Lucille's body lay.

"You are right," he spoke roughly. "She is dead."

He cursed the God of heaven for taking her life before he got there; then he started to leave but Jim stopped him.

"I want you to go ahead and place the mark on the body anyway. I just called the funeral home to come pick up the body and they informed me that they cannot do so unless it has the mark on it."

Sam walked back to the room with great satisfaction, because he would get to give her the mark anyway. The mark was placed on the cold forehead; but it meant nothing to Lucille, because her soul was already in eternity without God.

After Sam Fergus had gone, Jim sat down before the fireplace and fished out his mother's precious old Bible from where he had thrown it when he entered the house after taking the mark. Prompted by demon power, he began to tear the pages out of the Bible, one by one. After tearing a number of pages out, he ignited a match and kindled the pages. The flames leaped up and devoured the pages. Jim shouted with devilish glee as he tore page after page from the Bible and burned them.

"This damable Book will never decieve anyone else as it has me."

Jim did not realize that he could burn the pages of the Bible, but he could not purge himself of the Word that had been planted in his heart by a loving mother. God had spoken those words and they had life. Man speaks and many times his words die in a few moments after they are spoken, but God speaks and His words live on forever.

Amid many blasphemies and unheard-of oaths, Jim burned every page of Mother Collins' Bible—the Bible that had been her road map to heaven. It had solved many of her problems of life and had showed her the passage of escape from the horrible Tribulation Period.

Just as Jim finished destroying the last pages of the Word of God, he heard a terrible noise down the street. Jim's heart beat wildly in his bosom, because screams of many people were mixed with the noise. Racing to the window, he pulled back the curtain and his eyes searched anxiously for the meaning of all the excitement.

Suddenly, the most beautiful blood red horse came in sight. The rider wore a black suit, and he carried a long shining sword in his right hand waving it frantically. As suddenly as he had come, he was gone, dashing madly down the street.

Breathlessly, Jim stood waiting and wondering what would happen next; then he turned from the window and ran for the front porch. As far up and down the street as he could see, people were fighting among themselves. Everywhere the red rider went, he stirred people to war. It was a horrible scene to behold.

As the days passed, Jim realized the full meaning of the red horse and its rider. War had come to the nation. It was not a fairy tale, but it was real.

Great hatred was created in the hearts of those who had the mark to force everybody to take the mark or be put to death. Now, the days of persecution began for those who would not take the Mark of the Beast or worship him. Notices were tacked up throughout the city soliciting men for the Beast Regime to help rid the world of traitors and set up a lasting government of peace.

Jim read the poster and hurried to Calvin Heights to register. A number of men, all with the Mark of the Beast, had already arrived. They were ushered into a large room and seated around tables. The speaker, Launcelot Browning, was a swarthy, boisterous man with two, long, deep scars on his right cheek, and his eyes glittered and danced with demon power.

He spoke relentlessly and his hollow portentous voice rang out as he said, "Men, you have been called here for one main purpose and that is, as you have read on the posters, to rid the world of impostors and traitors. Our aim is to put the world under one government and make them like it. All people who call themselves Christians or who pray to any other God besides the Beast will be brought to headquarters and given a chance to recant. Everyone that we can get to surrender and become one of us will make us stronger. We will stand for no foolishness on their part. Do you understand?" he snarled.

"There are ways to make people change their minds or wish they had. No way of torture will be considered too cruel by this regime. The more cruel it is, the better. All the new ways you invent to torture these heretics and make them cry for mercy will be the better. You will be generously rewarded for your trouble. There is to be no mercy at all! If you let one person go free without taking the mark, whether it be friend or loved one, you will be put to death. We cannot let personal feelings stand in our way and do this work as the Beast demands it to be done; so empty yourself of all love and sympathy for anyone of your friends who might hold out on us.

"Now, men, you will find your uniforms in the next room. We want you to begin at once. Go out and round up every one who does not have the mark. They have had time to take it voluntarily if they wanted it. Now, we will use force. You will be paid, besides a regular salary, a premium for all you bring in.

"That is all. Go get your uniforms," Launcelot commanded and whirled on his heels and left the room.

Jim followed the rest of the men to the next room to receive his uniform. He felt proud of himself as he put on his uniform with gold buttons and bright glittering ensigns of the Mark of the Beast on the cap and each sleeve. A big, silver badge was pinned on the left lapel of his coat which gave him his power of authority in the regime of the Beast.

After all the men were dressed, they were told to go back to the room where they had received their first orders and line up to take the oath of the Beast Regime.

When all the men had entered the room and lined up, Launcelot Browning stood in front of them at

attention with his eyes looking straight ahead and
cried, "Attention! Fasten your eyes upon the image
of our god, raise your right hand and repeat after
me."

Each man solemnly, reverently and quietly did as
he was commanded. With a smirk on his lips he
began, and they followed all together with rhythm.

"I swear, by the Beast, that I will do all that is
within my power, to rid the world of impostors and
traitors. Every one who prays to or worships any
other God besides The Beast, I will spill my own blood,
if necessary, to convert him, or if he will not accept
the Beast, I will put him to death. I will show no
mercy; but, I will, with the authority invested in me,
hail men to prison and torture them until they surrender or die."

"You can lower your hand," he said sternly. "Now
we come to the last step."

From a gold jug on a near by table, he poured red
liquid into a gold goblet overlaid with diamonds, sap-
phires, jasper, and other precious stones.

"This is the blood of a Christian who was killed
yesterday because he would not give up his faith in
his so-called God and worship the Beast," he said
proudly. "As this is passed around, each man will
take a sip; and in the name of the Beast, we pray
that you will be blood-thirsty for the blood of all
Christians and sympathizers."

A gun strapped on one hip, a shining sword on the
other and a shrill whistle hanging from a gold chain

attached to a button hole in the shirt, completed their outfit. They were now ready to begin the blood curdling cry of honor and glory to the Beast.

They hurried from the room, anxious to do the Beast a service, and they went from house to house searching diligently for those who did not have the mark or were not making any effort to get it. The deadline of mercy that had been set by the Beast was now up.

Many men and women were hailed into prison and given a chance to recant and take the mark; but if they refused, the torturers began their work. People without the mark standing back in the shadows of some building in a secluded spot were petrified at the scenes of horror they witnessed.

Many people who were in a lukewarm condition at the time the rapture took place fell down before God and confessed they had failed Him and wanted to receive forgiveness. Backsliders sought the face of God and prayed until the blood of the Son of God had covered their souls. Sinners stirred by the coming of the Son of God found forgiveness for their sins. Now, all of them were having to seal their testimonies with their own blood.

It was a pathetic scene as audacious men led helpless men and women to their deaths. Iron posts with chains attached were erected for the purpose of burning the heretics. One could not help being seized by a sad feeling that was not easily shaken off after watching a saint of God being led to the stake with his face aglow and hearing his defiant, "No! I will never worship the Beast or his image! The God of heaven and Him only will I worship!"

When chained to the stake and the wood piled around him, he was asked again, "Will you take the mark?"

The answer without a flinch was, "No!"

Then, gas was poured on the wood until it was soaked, and the victim was asked for the last time if he would renounce his faith in his God.

Again the answer would come emphatically, "No! Never!"

With a ferocious oath, the fire was kindled, and the red flames licked hungrily around the victim. The saint, with a bewildered, frightened look, tried to keep from crying out, but the screams of agony automatically escaped his parched lips.

While men full of the devil gathered around and gave honor and glory to the Beast, souls were lifted and carried by angelic beings to that Celestial City whose builder and maker is God.

Juliana Ketner, a young girl about seventeen years of age, was brought out and given a chance to save herself by falling down and worshiping the image of the Beast.

Sobbingly she said, "No, I won't!" I won't!"

She was strapped around a pole with heavy wire like a hog that was about to be barbecued. The fire was kindled, the blaze soared high, and then she was held over the flames until all the life was gone from her body. She squirmed and tried to free herself, but it was of no use. Her screams echoed and re-echoed. Those watching from the shadows could hardly keep from running to her rescue, but they realized that they could not free her because she was surrounded by guards.

Many helpless Christians were thrown to the lions. Breathlessly, people watched from their places of hiding while the cruel men of the Beast Regime led men and women toward the den of ferocious lions. They listened to the roar of the angry lions as they waited impatiently for their prey. The soldiers always paused at the door of the den and asked their victims if they would renounce their God. Most of the answers they received were no, and ruthless hands opened the door of the den and threw them in. Just one pitiful, heart-rending scream floated through the air and all was quiet except for the roar of the lions fighting over their prey.

The red horse rider, representing war, brought about the appearance of the black horse rider which represented famine. War always brings a scarcity of food, and many people starve to death.

As the rider on the beautiful black horse rode the earth, famine settled down upon it. People were starving by the thousands, and the streets were littered with their dead bodies. The bodies with protruding ribs were a sickening sight to look at as one walked down the street.

Mother Collins had told Jim about the story in the

Book of Kings of how Samaria was shut in and no one
was going outside the walls of the city and no one
was coming in. The enemy, Syria, had them surrounded and the people in the city were starving to
death.

There were two women who had a son each. One
woman said to the other, "Give thy son, that we may
eat him today and we will eat my son tomorrow," so
they boiled and ate that woman's son; but the next
day the other woman was not willing to stick by her
bargain and she had hidden her son away. The woman
who had killed her son the day before, went to the
king and told him the story about killing her son and
now the other one had hidden her son away, but the
old king was not able to help her.

"Jim," she said, "that is a terrible story, but there
is coming a time worse than that. The Bible tells us
that there never has been a time such as is going to
be during the Tribulation Period."

Jim saw people so hungry they ate human flesh,
bugs, worms, snakes, rats and anything they could
find that was eatable.

The powers of the Beast were so strong it did not
seem that God cared what happened to them. Many
could not get food, so they walked into one of the
little offices and took the mark.

CHAPTER IX

Hester went through many things during the first few months of the Tribulation. Disaster was everywhere and fear clutched at her heart every moment. The first days after the rapture were almost more than she could bear. Nancy, the best chum she ever had, and most of her dearest friends were caught away. The gnawing thought that she could have gotten ready to meet the Lord and missed all of this heartache was constantly hammering in her brain. Somehow the long, dreary days passed into weeks.

At night when she would lie down to sleep, it would be hours before she would fall into a deep slumber, and when she did, it was a troublesome rest because she continually dreamed about the rapture and her being left behind.

When the Alabesta *Tribune* came out with the picture of the Antichrist, Hester looked at it and shuddered. She stared into the face of a man with a fierce countenance which seemed to come to life. She trembled as she stared at his countenance and felt the influence of his picture.

The thought came to her that one day he would reveal himself, and what would she do when she was led to a place of punishment and asked if she would take the Mark of the Beast? If she took it she would be doomed, and if she refused it would mean death.

Death! That was such a horrible word to those who had not been ready to meet their Lord. Hester knew that she was not ready to die and that she could never take the mark of doom.

With strong determination in her heart, she walked down the street to the church she loved so dearly. The tears stung her eyes as she entered the building. She looked around anxiously for just one person to pray for her, but there was no one.

"To think," she sobbed, "the people were so interested in my finding the Lord, and I thought I had plenty of time. How the devil deceived me. Oh, why! why didn't I believe God's Word?" she sighed.

Hester stood behind the sacred desk and thought of the many sermons of warning from God that had been proclaimed to mankind from the place where she stood. She opened the big Bible on the desk and began to read. Passage after passage of Scripture she read, and then she tried to imagine that a song was being sung for an altar invitation. With tears flowing down her cheeks, she humbly knelt at the altar.

"Oh God," she cried, "I know I have sinned against Thee. I realize I did wrong by not getting ready to meet Your Son, Jesus. Please," she said falteringly, "I just read in Your Word that You are a merciful God. Please, God, save my soul."

The enemy of her soul stood by and whispered the Lord did not care for her any more and she could not be saved, but she prayed on. She must find Him. She could not live any longer without Him.

Then, out of the darkness came a glimmer of light. She felt the burden lift, and she felt as light as a feather on the inside. She shouted glory, for truly it was glory to find the Lord. He had forgiven her, and she was so unworthy to have waited until now.

Brushing the tears from her eyes, she walked out of God's house feeling the best she had ever felt. There was fear, trouble, and suffering on every hand, but in her heart she had a deep settled peace.

Frank and Susan were completely broken up over the saints of God being gone, and Frank continued to attend his clubs trying to throw off the misery and terrifying fear clutching at his heart. After leaving the club he would go home, slip away to his room, lock the door and read God's Word. After reading the terrible judgments that were to be sent upon the earth as recorded by John in the Book of Revelation, he would kneel and try to pray. Worse things were to come upon the earth, and he was just entering the beginning of sorrows. He must find God.

Susan's gang gathered and tried to make merry and go on with life as if nothing had ever happened, but things just did not run as smoothly. Some of the gang could not forget the coming of the Lord, but others hardened their hearts against it by trying to convince themselves that there was nothing to it. When the rapture was mentioned it always made trouble, and they parted after many sharp words. The gang finally broke up, and for Susan it was a relief.

One evening, Frank and Susan came home late after attending a lecture meeting. Hester was in the living room praying for the salvation of her mother and daddy when they opened the door softly, intending to tiptoe through the room and not disturb her. Just as they stepped into the room, the Spirit of the Lord moved upon them, and they fell upon their knees, and began to pray to the God of heaven for mercy. Their cloak of pretense was shed, and as Hester prayed for them the victory came. They arose with all the doubts gone and filled with the joy of salvation because they had found the Lord.

The daily papers were full of the great exploits of the Beast. He had great power and performed many wonderful miracles which brought him more and more followers. Thousands who had scoffed at the statement that he was the Son of God were convinced and became Beast followers. The Jews knew that the Redeemer of Israel would have great power, but not once did they think he would be as great as he was.

It was a terrifying time to Hester when the headlines of the paper screamed that the covenant had been broken with the Jews. The great superman who had amazed the world with his miracles had now revealed himself to be the God of the Jews and of all peoples of the world and not the Christ, the Redeemer of Israel.

The Jews forsook him after all the many things he had done for them. He had done more for them than anyone else. He had made it possible for them to erect the magnificent temple in Jerusalem and offer sacrifices as their forefathers did in days of old. The news reporter, writing in sympathy with the Beast, said they were dissatisfied because they did not get their way in everything, and the Beast said they would come back because he was God and they could not get along without him.

Hester knew the truth was that the Jews had been deceived in the beginning by thinking he was the Son of God. Now their eyes had been opened, and they were no longer in darkness. They recognized him to be just what he was—the Wicked One, the Son of Perdition.

There were pictures of the Jews with torture and fear on their faces fleeing from the Antichrist. Oh! the horror they must have felt when the Antichrist unveiled himself, and they realized that the real Christ had been crucified by their forefathers. In that hour they got a glimpse of Calvary—Calvary with all its suffering, reproach and shame; Calvary with its glory, honor, and redemption. All these horrors they are going through now could have been escaped if they had only known the lowly Nazarene was the Son of God.

As Hester glanced at the different pictures, she thought of the hundred and forty-four thousand Jews who were to be caught away to be with the Lord during the Tribulation Period. She knew they were the man child that was spoken of in the twelfth chapter of Revelation. The woman was Israel, and the man child consisted of twelve thousand men chosen by God from each of the twelve tribes which made one hundred and forty-four thousand.

In the fourteenth chapter of Revelation, Hester learned who the man child was. The Scripture said that the one hundred and forty-four thousand were all virgins because they had not been defiled by women, so Hester knew that the one hundred and forty-four thousand would have to be men. They were to be caught up during the Tribulation because John saw them in heaven, and the Tribulation was still going on. They were classed as the first fruits to God. Surely, she thought, they had been caught away by this time.

"How wonderful," she said, "to have been caught up to heaven out of this terrible time that is upon the earth. If only I can stand true to the Lord, one day my troubles will be over, too."

After the Mark of the Beast was introduced, images were set up in Alabesta. She was startled beyond words the first time she saw the image of the Beast. It was just an image, but it had power to speak. Spasmodically she watched as the people gathered around and worshiped the image. Her heart was pounding, and she panted for breath as she watched the unbelievable scene. She was appalled at the power the image had, and she could hardly keep from bowing down and worshiping it. She had to continually plead the blood of Jesus. Hester and others standing back without the mark made a poignant scene as they watched the image worshipers.

The sky was a beautiful blue with pink patches here and there, and the sun was shining; but there was nothing beautiful and warm to Hester. Her world had been turned upside down.

The Mark of the Beast was being discussed on every street corner.

"I will never take the mark if I starve," one said.

Another said, "I don't know yet just what I am going to do. We will have to do something to get food. We can't just starve."

Hester stood at the entrance of the largest super market in the city and she carefully scrutinized the market. Sure enough, as people passed the cashier, each one had to show the mark before the groceries were checked.

She was rigid from the top of her head to the soles of her feet as she watched a mere wisp of a lady struggling down the aisle to the cashier. From under her white starched bonnet, silvery curls glistened in the ray of light. Her face was lined with wrinkles, but a light shone in her eyes. She set her groceries down on the cashier's desk but made no move to show the mark.

Zandra, the cashier, carried the mark in her forehead. She glared at the little old lady with a suspicious look. Hester could tell from where she was standing that she was an austere person and would show no mercy.

"Come! Come!" Zandra snarled. "I don't have all day to wait on you. Where is the mark?"

The little old lady gave her a bewildered stare and did not make a move to show the mark. The line behind her was growing longer, and there was a restless feeling in the air as they waited impatiently to have their groceries checked.

"Do you or do you not have the mark?" Zandra drawled. "If you do, let me see it; and if you do not, get out of the way."

The eyes of everyone within earshot rested upon the little old lady as she lifted her head with a sad, troubled stare.

"No," she said with a faint whisper, "but please," she rushed on, "let me buy this once."

The answer came harsh and boisterous. "Indeed! I should say not! And just who do you think you are? Can't you read? Can't you see all the signs and notices tacked up around here that you need not select groceries unless you have the mark? Now beat it," she said with an oath, "before I call the police."

The old lady did not move. Her shoulders began to shake as she drew out a handkerchief from her pocket and wiped her eyes.

"Please, don't send me away without food. We don't have any at home."

"That's fine," Zandra sharply said. "Maybe you will come to your senses quicker and take the mark. Now, scram!" she said, removing her groceries from the counter.

The old lady did not move a muscle, but her eager gaze still rested on the tyrant cashier.

With this, the cashier went into a rage. "So you are just a half-witted old fool who cannot read or understand plain English. We have another remedy to use on ignorant people like you," she fumed.

By this time an officer had arrived who had cruel eyes like all of those who had the mark. The officer had the mark in his forehead and the ensign of the mark on his sleeve and cap. Roughly he seized the old lady by the arm and pulled her toward the door. She was petrified with horror and began to call on God to help her as the defiant officer took her away.

Hester turned and fled from the store, wiping her tears because she realized the little old lady was a child of God. What a pity the old lady had not been ready when the Lord came. She would have been saved all these heartaches.

Groping and stumbling with tears blinding her way, Hester came to a crowd gathered in front of the bank door. Patrol cars were parked at the curb in front. Just as Hester arrived, the officers were dragging a man to the car with bloody, torn clothes. He had been beaten terribly.

"It's my money!" he cried, "and I intend to get it!"

"Oh, no, you won't unless you take the mark!" one officer declared vehemently.

Hester gasped. Her hand flew to her mouth to stiffle a scream that was on the verge of escaping, and her face turned deathly pale. One of the officers was Mother Collins' Jim, and he had the Mark of the Beast!

"Oh, no!" she choked under her breath. "It can't be Mother Collins' son!"

Then before she realized what she was doing, she cried out, "Jim! Jim Collins!"

The officer with a mop of black, wavy hair, big broad shoulders and features that would have been handsome had it not been for the sneer on his lips and the glitter of demon power in his dark eyes, whirled on his heel and glared down into Hester's eyes.

"Who are you?" he commanded.

Hester had lost her power of speech for the moment, but finally managed to stammer, "I—I—am—Hester—Bell—Wilson."

She felt frozen on the inside. Was she going to die? She must get hold of herself, she thought. This would never do.

"I—I—went—to the same church—your mother went to. She was a dear—dear—friend of mine. The best friend I ever had." She stopped with a sob.

When she mentioned Jim's mother's name, he began to seethe and his body shook with hatred.

"Don't!" he cried, gritting his teeth and letting out a terrible oath. "Don't you ever dare mention her name to me again!" he said, clenching his fist as if he was going to strike her. "I have shut her out of my mind completely and now you are reminding me of her! I hate her! I hate her! Do you understand?" he shouted. "I loathe the ground she walked on."

He cursed his fate of being brought up by such an old-fogyish mother.

"I despise her for the rotten superstition she taught me. Now, she is so foolish as to have hidden herself away trying to make me believe she has been caught away by her God. It's all a damnable lie."

"Stop!" Hester shouted, forgetting the danger she was putting herself in. "You cannot talk about Mother Collins like that! I won't let you," she cried hysterically.

By this time she was blocking his path and pulling him frantically by his coat. Jim shook her off and gave her a beastly kick.

"Away with you, you dog!" he exclaimed.

He started to strike her again, but she drew back and was lost in the crowd. She heard him shout, "Stop that girl! She is mad!" and that was all she remembered.

Somehow she got away from that scene of anguish, but she never knew how.

When she came to herself, she was in the park behind some thick shrubbery, sobbing her heart out. At first, she thought she had gone to sleep and dreamed all of what had really happened. She started to stand to her feet, wondering how she had gotten there and why she had decided to take a nap; then she fell back on the grass with a low moan. Her leg was hurt so badly; it throbbed with misery.

Her mind was clear. It was not a dream but a dreadful reality. Mother Collins' Jim had sold his soul to the devil and had said all those harsh things about his wonderful mother, and kicked her. Mother Collins would never see her Jim again. He had no chance of heaven now. He was like a demon from hell. Why did he do it?

Hester shuddered, and more determination than ever entered her heart to resist taking the mark, even if she starved or was tortured to death.

The days that followed were days of uncertainty for those who did not have the Mark of the Beast. They had to be very cautious, because any moment they might be asked to open their right hand and produce the mark. More and more, people were being put to death because they would not renounce the Christ of God and take the mark. Hester often wondered how much longer her family would be able to escape. Officers of the Beast Regime were going from house to house, hailing men and women to prison. If they took the mark, they were released; but if they did not, they were taken to a place of torture.

Lying along the streets dead bodies of people who had starved to death without taking the mark, sent a feeling of triumph through Hester because she knew that that was one more the Beast could not make recant and take his mark. Death was not an unwelcome visitor to Hester any more. She felt it would be a relief to lie down and die. Many times she had prayed to die, but God had not seen fit to grant her petition.

One day while Hester was at home alone, there came a loud rap on the door. Breathlessly she waited. What would be the best thing to do? Her mother and father had gone out to find food. Food was a real problem to get because neither of them had taken the Mark of the Beast.

There was another loud knocking and a gruff voice said, "Open up in the name of the Beast."

The blood was drained from Hester's face, and she looked around for a place to hide, but there was none. What could she do?

The commanding voice came again. "Open up or we will break the door down!"

Her heart pounded madly. She knew she had no choice. She must open the door.

Quickly snatching up the Bible, she hid it under one of the cushions on the sofa and prayed, "Dear God, help me to be calm and direct my words." Then, she opened the door.

"I think it is about time," said the officer with the gruff voice. "What has kept you so long?" he demanded, giving her a searching look.

"Won't you please come in," she said with a polite tone of ease.

The three officers did not wait for further invitation, but they stomped into the house as if it were a barn to house animals.

"Sit down," Hester invited, with a calm sweet voice.

A great storm was going on inside her body. Would her mother and daddy come before these men left; and if so, what would they do to them? What could she tell them when they asked about the mark? Many pressing questions were stampeding her brain for an answer. Frantically, she tried to think of appropriate answers for the questions she felt certain were about to be asked.

"Who lives here beside you?" the shortest of the three sharply asked.

"My mother and daddy," she replied, lifting her chin.

"Do all of you have the mark?" he asked, his eyes resting upon her.

She did not flinch, but with a clear, steady voice she answered, "I don't."

In her heart she prayed, "God let this throw them off the track so they will not ask if mother and daddy have the mark."

"Why don't you?" he questioned, coming closer to her.

"Because it is not right for me to take it," she said, looking straight into his eye.

"What do you mean it is not right for you to take the mark?" he asked, annoyed at her innocent stare.

"I mean I am a Christian," she boldly replied.

Her face glowed with the ardent love of her Redeemer. All the fear was gone from her heart.

"I have been bought with a great price—something more precious than silver or gold."

"What could that be?" one interrupted with a snap. "Don't speak in riddles, my fair lady. Tell us so we can understand."

"Indeed, I will tell you," Hester humbly said. "It is the blood of the Son of God."

Immediately, all the pity for her was gone from their eyes. It was true she made a beautiful picture as she stood before them, but when she proclaimed her faith in another God besides the Beast, they forgot everything but their love and loyalty for the god they served.

Blaspheming the name of the God of heaven, they swore they would take that silly notion out of her head. Raging with anger they began pulling open the desk drawers and throwing things on the floor. They marched into the bedroom and began pulling out the dresser drawers. Hester followed them and watched with despairing eyes as they tossed her mother's things here and there.

When they started to mount the stairs, Hester stopped them by saying, "I guess you are looking for the Word of God."

The men looked amazed and one answered abruptly, "We are looking for that damnable Book called the Bible. You might call it the Word of God, but we do not. If there is one of those Books here, we will find it or tear up the entire place."

"There is not a Bible up there. I put my Bible under one of the cushions of the sofa in the parlor."

They stared at her incredulously. They had never met a girl like her. What a blessing she would be to the Beast Regime if they could change her belief. That was what they needed—people who were not afraid of anything, and that girl was not. From the first moment they laid eyes on her, she had been composed.

With eyes filled with hatred for God's Word, one officer rushed to the place of hiding and a rough hand pulled it irreverently from its place of hiding. To Hester's surprise, they did not tear it to shreds as she had thought they would do.

With a cunning look, one of the men told Hester to hold out her hands. She willingly obeyed, and as she held out two milky white hands, a pair of shining handcuffs were snapped on her wrists, but she did not show any emotion.

"Come with us." The command was given with a cold smile by the one who seemed to be the leader of the three.

Hester walked out of her home not expecting ever to be back again, but she was seeking a city whose builder and maker is God. She glanced around hurriedly, painting the familiar scenes upon her brain.

She held her head high as she walked down the street between two guards, one following. She knew she was going to her death, but one day Jesus started on the death march to Calvary for her. What a privilege it was to die for His sake. He had done so much for her.

No one spoke until they were half way down the block; then Hester broke the silence when she noticed how her Bible was being treated by the audacious man who carried it.

With a sweet mellow voice she pleaded, "Will you please let me carry my Bible until we get there?"

"Indeed not!" one of the officers blazed, giving her a rough shove.

The one who carried it was anxious to please Hester as he was determined to win her for the Beast

Regime. He had no intentions of putting her to death unless she continued to be stubborn. She was so young he did not feel he would have much trouble with her.

"I don't see why she should not since we have to take it in, and I am sure I do not care to carry the filthy thing. It makes cold sweat pop out on my brow. I was just thinking of making one of you fellows carry it."

That was enough to settle the argument. Neither of the other two had any desire to carry the horrible old Book. No matter how calm they tried to be, it always unnerved them to carry that Book.

The Bible with its soft, flexible covers was placed under Hester's arm, and she hugged it to her heart. It felt warm, and she could feel strength flowing from it to her body. She felt calmer on the inside, because she could feel the assurance that God would be with her, even in death.

Finally, they came to a red brick building. In the yard were devices that were used to torture Christians. Someone was being burned at the stake just as Hester and the officers entered, and a crowd had gathered around to watch it well done. The foul odor of burning human flesh filled her nostrils, and she became nauseated. One glance, and she knew the soul had already taken its flight from the body.

The officers ushered her into a large room before a desk where a man sat with wicked eyes that made her want to draw back in horror.

"Will you take the mark?" asked the man behind

the desk. "It will save you a lot of trouble, and you can walk out free if you will take it. It is such a simple act," he continued with deceit playing in his eyes, "and you are too young to die."

He gave her a pat on the hand, but she drew back as if a snake had struck at her.

"We can use a girl like you in the Beast Regime. We need sensible people who know how to be calm in the midst of trouble," he said, trying to use a channel of duplicity to win her for the Beast. "I am sure you saw the unpleasant scene outside which is very regrettable, but people must be made to realize that the Beast is not one to play with and that he means business. Shall we give you the mark, or would you prefer the same fate?"

Hester lifted her head with dignity, and her answer came with a frank, clear tone, "No! I will never take the mark."

The three officers stared in unbelief. Had their ears heard right? What kind of supernatural power had charge of this girl that caused her to fear nothing—not even death?

The face of the man behind the desk became livid with rage, and he commanded with a harsh voice, "Take her away! I think we have a few experiments that will help her change her mind."

He scrawled an order and handed it to one of them.

Rough hands seized her and she was marched through the back door and down a narrow, dingy hall with cells on either side.

"This order says put her in one of the front cells

where she will have a nice view of the scenery," he said with mocking laughter that made Hester's blood run cold.

She was pushed through an opening with a huge iron door; then the door was slammed, and the key turned in the lock. For a moment she stood looking at the door that had been closed behind her, then she turned her eyes and looked around. There was only one piece of furniture: a dirty old cot with a couple of filthy blankets thrown carelessly across it. The cell had one small window with heavy bars. Peering between the bars into the courtyard where people who would not worship the Beast were being tortured, she saw the charred and smoking body of a dear old saint of God who had sealed his testimony with his blood. Hester trembled as she viewed the nauseating scene and clung to the bars of the window for support.

"My God!" she prayed, "help me to be strong and die the victorious death."

Hester heard noises and was aware that other people were locked in the prison besides her. She was not able to see them, because the door was a solid piece of iron and the cement walls reached within two feet of the ceiling with iron bars finishing out the other two feet of space. Eagerly, she listened for a familiar voice, but the moans and cries of different ones praying was all she could hear.

Hester still clutched her Bible under her arm. Surely it was a miracle of God that they had forgotten to notice the Bible before they locked her up. Hastily, she hid it under the dirty cot, thanking God that He had been so thoughtful as to let her keep her precious Bible. It was more than she could have ever hoped for. How terrible to be in a place like this, but what a wonderful consolation to know that the Lord was thoughtful of her.

Over the moans and cries from other prisoners, she heard the huge bell in the courtyard dolefully ringing. She knew what that meant, because she had heard it many times before and witnessed the aftereffects They were going to send another heretic to a martyr's grave. Her heart hammered in her bosom. Was she the one that was about to die?

Then she heard footsteps. Her hand flew to her mouth to stop the scream that was about to escape through frightened lips. There was a swift flutter of garments outside, then the clattering of a key as it was thrust into the lock of her door. She stood pale as paste. She knew her time had come. The door was cautiously opened and a man stood there with a sword in his hand as if he were ready to take her life right then. For a moment he glared at her with his piercing, black eyes lighted up like coals of fire. Hester was petrified with fear and she tried to move forward and say, "I am ready," but not a sound would come.

The man broke the silence, saying with a furious tone which no one would dare disobey, "You are to go over and stand at the window. Under no circumstances are you to move. Do you understand?" he sharply asked. "There is a beautiful scene that we want you to see. Go! as you are commanded to do!" he shouted with an oath.

Hester moved as one in a trance. It did not seem real. This could not be happening to her. Stumbling blindly to the window, she looked out into the court-yard; then the door was shut with a bang, and the key turned in the lock. Sobs coming from a short distance away reached her ear, and she knew she was not the only one that was being forced to watch the death of a saint.

Many shouts went up to the Beast from the crowd gathered in the courtyard; then suddenly everything became quiet, and a few moments of tense waiting followed. Footsteps rang heavily outside her cell door. She listened. On down the hall they tramped; then a pause, a rattling of keys, and the big, squeaky iron gate leading to the courtyard was opened.

In a few moments the captain of the guards cried. "Attention!" with a loud, rough voice. The guards made a double line on each side of a large, circular iron lid. That must be a new way of torture, she thought. Her knuckles turned a pale blue from the tense strain of clinging to the bars.

A beautiful, frail, young woman was pushed sav-agely down between the two lines of soldiers by a crude, giant of a man. Her golden blond hair glis-tened in the sunlight, making a beautiful background for her milky complexion. Her eyes had the glow of Divine glory. Her lips quivered slightly, but that was the only sign of fear. Her shoulders were held erect with a sweet dignity that no one watching could help but admire. The cruel guard did not push her the last few yards, and she walked slowly. How were they going to kill her, or would they kill her at all? Would she recant at the last moment and renounce her faith in God?

"Oh merciful God," Hester prayed, "please give her strength to give her life for Your sake."

Just then, two men raised the lid from a large, deep pit. From the window, Hester could see far enough down into the pit to see the black, poisonous, slimy snakes of many different kinds crawling over each other. Her eyes flew wide, and she cringed in horrid terror as she saw what the young woman's fate was going to be. Cold sweat formed on her brow while icy chills ran up and down her spine. The lady was made to stand at the side of the pit so the prisoners could see the horror on her face when she perceived her destiny.

The young lady's eyes were wide in horror as she was forced to look down into the den of snakes. Their heads were lifted to the victim, and their forked tongues ran out of their mouths furiously.

Hester felt an urge to scream, but she knew she must control herself. Like a shadow, she vanished from the barred window and fell upon the floor, shaking with sobs.

Immediately, a guard was at the window saying with an oath, "Hey, you in there, get yourself back at this window as you have been commanded. Who do you think you are anyway? Take it from me, lady, if you are wise, you will obey orders, and they will not have to be given the second time either," he snarled.

With trembling, weak legs that did not seem sufficient to stand on, Hester crept back to the window just in time to hear a guard say to the young woman, "Will you renounce your faith and take the Mark of the Beast, declaring from this day on that he is the true and only god?"

The woman stood there like a marble stone without lowering an eyelid. Everything was so quiet it was like a graveyard. All eyes were focused on her, waiting for an answer. The woman did not hesitate to give her desire.

"No!" she said without a flinch. "I will never recant. There is only one God. The God I serve," she emphatically said, "is the God of the universe."

The guard glared at her and began pushing her slowly and closer toward the edge of the pit hoping she would recant at the last second. Then the guard, with a shout of honor to the Beast, gave the woman a sudden shove, and into the pit she fell giving the most pitiful scream Hester had ever heard—one that would haunt her as long as she lived.

The woman screamed again and again as the mad serpents hissed and bit her. A large boa constrictor coiled its huge body around hers, and her last scream was followed by a choking sound as the slimy snake squeezed the life from her body. The noise subsided, the pit lid lowered, and the Beast worshipers fell on on their knees giving honor and glory to the Beast.

That was all Hester remembered until some hours later she came to lying on the floor. Her head felt as if it were bursting. Where was she, and what had happened to her? Then the beastly death she had witnessed came back to her with maddening force.

"I must have fainted," she murmured, pulling herself to a sitting position.

A groan escaped her lips. She was sore and stiff all over as if she had been beaten. For a long time she sat on the floor not caring if she died. Life was not worth living any more. If only she was out of it all.

The sun had set in the west, and the late eventide was casting long shadows in Hester's room. The key turned in the lock, and the door was opened revealing the same guard with the wicked twinkle in his eyes.

"Here," he grunted, handing her a tin pan with some cold beans and a stale piece of bread. Then he gave her a tin cup filled with water and, warning her, he said, "You better be saving with this because you will be given just a very small amount each day."

Before Hester had time to say anything, he turned and marched toward the door with an air of importance.

With an afterthought he suddenly turned, faced her and asked with a tone of mockery, "By the way, how did you like the wonderful service we had this afternoon?" His eyes glittered with demon power as he watched her intently. Then with a sneer he reminded her, "You had better change your mind before a worse thing happens to you," then locked the door.

It was hard to swallow any of the meager allowance of food, but she knew it would be better for her physical condition if she could eat something.

That night as she lay on the rickety, old cot under filthy blankets, many thoughts crowded her mind. Two, big tears rolled down her cheeks as she thought of her mother and daddy. What would be their fate? Did they know by now where she was? She knew her daddy would try to rescue her even at the risk of his own life.

Humbly she prayed to God to help him not to do anything drastic.

Through the darkness, she could see the white face of the woman and her eyes wide with fright as she was being pushed into the pit of snakes. Those screams rang over and over in her mind. Oh, the spasms of horror she felt, and she tried to blot them out of her mind.

Finally, after many hours of tossing from one side of the cot to the other, she fell asleep only to dream of snakes coiling around her body and blood curdling screams of a woman.

What a relief it was when the night was over and another day had dawned. What the day held for her she did not know, but at least the black night with its hideous blackness had vanished.

CHAPTER X

Frank and Susan came home shortly after the three officers left with Hester. They were shocked beyond words when they found the house in a topsy-turvy condition and Hester gone. The thing they had feared so long had come. What could they do? Hester was young, and they might persuade her to take the mark or trick her into taking it. Both of them were wild with anxiety. There was no doubt in their minds that Hester had been taken by the Beast Regime. If they only knew what to do for the best. They agreed it would be better to wait until after dark before they went in search of her.

As they were about to sit down to eat a few bites of some cold, left over food, there came a light knock at the back door. Susan's heart missed a beat.

She looked at her husband, and with trembling lips she whispered with a low, shaky voice, "Who do you suppose it is?"

"I don't know," Frank answered with a husky voice, staring at the door as the knock continued getting louder.

Petrified with horror, Susan watched as her husband cautiously opened the door a few inches and peered into the darkness.

"Frank," Jack Rand said; then the door was swung wide.

With a sigh of relief Susan sat back in her chair. Jack Rand was a close friend whom they had helped to find the Lord the day before.

Breathlessly, he told them that he had seen three officers of the Beast Regime take Hester up the street that afternoon. Susan wept aloud as he told how boldly she walked with her Bible under her arm.

Revenge sprang up in Frank's heart. He felt like taking his gun and murdering every person he could find who had the mark. Susan noticed the dreadful look on his face. Frank must not lose his head and do something drastic. They must be guided by the Spirit and do the right thing.

"Frank, let's kneel and take it to our heavenly Father. He will know what we should do."

On the kitchen floor the three knelt before the Lord and poured their hearts out, asking for wisdom and strength to do the will of the Almighty. They arose with renewed hope and courage after some time had passed, and the benignant visitor left after promising he would earnestly pray for Hester to be delivered or stand true to God until the end.

Night had settled down with its thick, black blanket, and Frank Wilson stood outside the gate which led to the courtyard of the prison watching furtively for a chance to pass the guards. He must get by, even at the risk of his own life. Hester was locked in that prison somewhere if they had not killed her already. The thought of Hester being put to death by cruel hands urged him to take a greater chance. Love for her and her well-being drove away the fear for his own life.

After what seemed an hour, he saw his chance to sneak through. The two guards at the gate had been arguing, and suddenly arms and fists began to fly. In their fury they forgot their duty, and that is how Frank managed to slip through the gate unnoticed.

Trying to stay out of sight of the eyes of anyone who might be in the courtyard or come out of the prison door, he moved silently forward along the shadowed wall, until he passed the front part of the building and came in sight of the cells with their barred windows. Looking all around and seeing no one, he made a dash for the cells. He panted loudly with excitement and exertion when he reached the building. Crouching in the shadows of the building, again he waited, but there was not a sound except the moans of suffering humanity on the other side of the barred windows.

Moving like a fox with his body hugging the wall, he came to the first window. Sheltering his eyes with his hand, he peered into the cell. There were numbers of prisoners in that cell. Some were sprawled on the floor, some sitting, and others standing.

Looking all around him, he called softly, "Hester, honey, are you in there?"

Every muscle in his body was tense as he waited and wondered if anyone was going to answer him. A number of faces appeared at the window trying to see out.

"Is my daughter, Hester, in there?" he asked anxiously.

A woman turned from the window and asked with a sweet, mellow voice, "Is there anyone in here named Hester? If so, someone out here wants to see you."

All shook their heads and the woman turned her face back toward the window and answered, "No."

With a heavy heart, he moved on to the next window. His eyes searched the cell but there was no woman in that cell.

Haggard, he moved on to the next one. He heard a groan and his heart jumped with excitement. It was Hester! He looked through the iron bars into the narrow cell. A ray of light from the dingy hall fell upon the seraphic face of Hester as she lay upon the cot under the dirty blankets dreaming of snakes and people being put to death.

Just as he started to call her, he heard footsteps. He listened! His rapid breathing could be heard for some distance in the stillness as he huddled against the wall frightened; not for his own safety as much as for Hester's. What would become of Hester if he were taken?

The footsteps were getting louder which meant the night watchman was getting closer and coming in that direction. Then, around the corner came a guard carrying a large flashlight shining it in all directions. His light moved slowly down the wall of the building until it rested on Frank. He was frozen with dismay as the light was shined into his face and a gruff voice spoke.

"Come out from there before I blow you into smithereens."

Frank felt numb all over as he staggered toward the defiant guard who held a gun in one hand and a light in the other.

"So you have come to take the mark, uh?" the man grunted with a mocking sneer. "That is just dandy. It will save us the trouble of going out and bringing you in."

Giving Frank a hard kick, he pushed him ahead of him with the nozzle of the gun pressed against his back. When they reached the front door, he bade Frank open it. The light that flooded the darkness as the door was opened, blinded Frank, and for a moment he hesitated. The guard gave him another violent kick which sent him staggering into the room.

"Just look what I found in me own back yard," the guard remarked with a jubilant chuckle. "A lover, I guess, who came to keep a date with his best girl but was interrupted by a cruel papa before he got gone."

The man behind the desk glared at Frank. "What were you doing outside that cell window?" he asked acidly. "We don't like lovers around here."

Frank's blood boiled with indignation and before he thought he blurted out, "That happens to be my daughter!"

The men were astounded at the statement.

"Oh," the maid said with a wink at the guard who had brought Frank in. "This is interesting. So papa tells daughter to take the mark."

"I will never advise my daughter to take the mark and sell her soul to the devil," Frank said with stern boldness. "I pray to God that she will be strong enough to withstand all your brutal tortures and die a victorious death embracing the true faith."

The man behind the desk went almost insane with rage.

"Stop it, you fool!" he shouted with glittering eyes. "That is blasphemy! Any more of that kind of talk and I will have you killed this night! If this girl is your daughter, where is your wife?"

"My wife is not with me," Frank replied quickly to avoid telling the whereabouts of his wife.

"I am no fool," the man said with a dark frown. "I can see that she is not with you, but you are going to tell us where she is, so you may just as well start now before we have to put you through the third degree. We have ways of making smart guys like you talk. The Beast is the true god of the universe and you will obey him. Do you understand?" he said scornfully.

"I will obey God," Frank answered without flinching.

He was led away to a room of torture, and the punishment began. They tortured him in many ways, but he would not tell where his wife was; but somehow they learned the location of his home. Frank never knew how they secured the information.

After they had tortured him many hours, Susan was brought in. When she saw her husband, she gave a scream of surprise.

"What have you done to him?" she sobbed, rushing to his side.

His face was swollen, both eyes black, his shirt torn from his back, and merciless hands had beaten him until they tired.

"Oh, we just been giving him a little beauty treatment," one said laughingly, amused at his own joke.

Then a frown came over his face, and he looked straight at Susan with wicked eyes which made her most miserable and said, "We are going to give him worse than that if he doesn't get some sense in his head and learn to take orders. If you are wise, you will do as you are told. Let your husband's misfortune be a lesson to you."

They were led away to a musty cell, and as the guard locked the door, he said with a pitiless voice, "The lady who occupied this cell won't need it any longer. They didn't only roast her alive, but she was burned to a crisp."

Seeing their agony, he gave a hideous laugh as he slammed and locked the door.

The sun was shining through Hester's cell window when she awoke the next morning, and her heart rejoiced because the long, dreadful night had ended.

There was the rattling of a key in the lock, and her face paled. With trembling hands, she hurriedly tucked her Bible under the thin mattress.

When the guard entered the room, he found her with her back turned to the door, and she was looking out of the small window. The guard spoke to her with mocking kindness in his voice. She whirled around suddenly as if she were not aware of his presence in the room until he spoke. He acted rather friendly as he set her breakfast on the floor and asked her if she had rested well and some other questions, but Hester was in no mood to talk; and when she did answer, she spoke in a crisp, uninterested manner.

The breakfast was warm and very appetizing. Why had they suddenly changed their attitude toward her? She felt sure that it was not for the sake of love or sympathy; nevertheless, she ate it ravenously, for she was very hungry. The guard did not make a move to leave, so Hester just ignored him and ate her breakfast.

Just as she had about finished eating, there were footsteps, and she looked up into the face of the captain of the guards. Like a flash, the guard who had brought her breakfast stood at attention with his hand raised to his head making the salute of the Beast Regime.

"The Beast live forever."

"How is my young lady today?" the captain asked kindly, coming closer to Hester.

"I am very well, thank you," Hester answered serenely.

"I would delight in giving the order to have you released from this unpleasant place. Such a sweet girl like you has no business being locked in a place like this. If you will just do one little thing, which is very simple, I can order your freedom at once."

Hester did not respond to his flattery. She sat composed and gave him an uninterested stare. The captain frowned. This was not working as he had anticipated. He thought surely by this time Hester would be anxious to get out of this hole and would jump at his offer.

"Now, young lassie, all you have to do is just take a little simple mark that does not hurt at all and will be quickly over with."

He saw the strong resentment written on her face as she said calmly, "I will never take the mark. Do to me whatever you will. My Bible tells me not to fear the one who can destroy the body, but the one who can destroy both soul and body. I am not interested in your offers now or later. The answer will always be the same—no."

For a moment, the captain stared at her in disbelief. Could he have heard right? This helpless girl surely could not have turned down his offer so quickly. He had been confident that he could get her to change her mind with a little kindness and sympathy. He had showed her kindness by having her served a nice, warm breakfast of the best food he could get, and she had returned his kindness like an ungrateful enemy. How the boys would laugh at him. Oh, they would not dare laugh in front of him, but when he had his back turned, they would wink at each other and laugh gleefully because this young girl had not bowed to his will.

That thought drove him into a fit of blasphemies. His hands itched to take her white, creamy throat into their strong grip and choke the life from her body. A plan came to him while he was prancing with rage from one end of the narrow cell to the other. The more he thought about it, the calmer he became; and self-assurance was his again.

"Maybe it would be interesting to you to know that your mother and daddy were brought in last night."

Hester's eyes flew wide with bewilderment, and her cold lips parted.

"I thought you might be interested," he said mockingly.

The guard followed the captain, and they left her alone in the dreary, cold cell. Hester felt like a caged animal as she stood at the window gripping the bars and looking into the distance. Mother and daddy had been brought in. What would their fate be? If only there was something she could do to help them escape. It did not matter about her, but the thought of her own sweet mother and daddy being in the hands of those cruel men was agitating. What if they should make them recant for her sake?

"Please, God, help them to be strong," she prayed earnestly with tears spilling down her rose petal cheeks.

The next few hours were hours of torture as she waited anxiously for more word about her mother and daddy. Thousands of dark thoughts passed through her mind as the morning slowly passed. She listened intently every time she heard footsteps, but each time they would die away and no one came to the cell.

About noon, heavy footsteps rang out on the cement floor of the hall, and then they paused in front of her cell. The door was opened, and the same guard who had brought her breakfast came in.

"Your father asked me to give this to you," he said with a friendly smile and handed her a note.

"Thank you," she said, quickly grasping the thin piece of paper.

With trembling hands she hurriedly unfolded the note and read the startling contents:

My dear child,

I imagine you have been very anxious about your mother and me, but you need not be troubled any longer. We are all right; in fact, we are happier than we have ever been in all our life. We have taken the Mark of the Beast. We had been deceived, but now we have found the true light. Your mother and I are anxiously waiting for the news that you have taken the mark, too. Please don't disappoint us and then we can all be together again. Remember, we both love you dearly.

Affectionately,
Daddy

Her mother and daddy had taken the Mark of the Beast, and now they wanted her to take it?

"No! No!" she shrieked hysterically. "It can't be! It can't be!"

She looked up into the guard's eyes, and with tears rolling down her cheeks she pleaded like a small child, "Please tell me it is not true. Tell me my daddy didn't write this."

The guard looked at her sadly and said with a helpless gesture, "I am afraid it is true. Your daddy gave me that note himself. You can see that it is in his own handwriting."

She glanced down at the note. Yes, it was her daddy's writing.

"How could they have done it?" she sobbed aloud. "I have prayed so many times for them not to fail."

The guard still remained in the cell, but Hester did not care what she said. It did not matter to her if he did have the mark. She was beyond caring. Oh, the thought that her mother and daddy had become weak and sold their souls to the devil made her want to scream as loud as she could and never cease screaming.

Her daddy's request was that she take the mark also. The thought made Hester shudder. Take the mark? No! She would never take the mark. Not even . . . no, not even at the persuasion of her own parents.

"My God," she cried, "now we will never be a happy family because mother and daddy are denied heaven."

The ordeal was too much for Hester and she gave a pitiful cry like a wounded animal and fainted. The guard picked her up and carried her to the office.

When Hester came to, the captain was bending over her.

"Everything will be all right now," he whispered in her ear.

Hester struggled to get to her feet, but at first she was not able. After getting to her feet, she wrung her hands together in despair as the cruel reality came rushing over her like a mighty wave in the deep.

The captain said, "Now I feel sure you are ready to take the mark, because you want to make your mother and daddy happy. Take the mark, and you will be free. You will not have to go back to that old cell another time," he said tenderly, placing his hand on her shoulder.

Hester withdrew from him and said, "No! No! I will never take the mark! I am indeed sorry that my mother and daddy have taken the mark, but I cannot fail my God just because they have," she humbly said, panting for breath.

She looked straight into the captain's eye with her eyes shining with the glory of God and continued. "No matter what you do to me, I will never take the mark."

"Very well," he said roughly. "If this is the way you want it, we will see. You have not been tortured yet. People can talk plenty pretty when they are not in any pain. I thought you could be changed through your parents, but you don't have that much love for them. You are not human," he said with an oath.

He motioned to two guards, and they disappeared. Hester waited breathlessly, wondering what they were going to do to her. Then the door through which the two guards had disappeared opened, and there stood her mother and daddy.

"Mother! Daddy!" she cried, pulling away from the guard and rushing over to them. "Why did you take the mark?" she asked pleadingly.

Her parents were aghast.

"We haven't taken the mark, child," they both said, puzzled. "What do you mean?"

"Daddy didn't you write me a note saying you and mother had taken the mark and desired me to take it?" she asked, looking up into his face questioningly.

"No, child," he answered through swollen lips that had been beaten. "I haven't written you a note. They have tried to trick you into taking the mark."

Before more could be said, Hester was pulled away from her parents. Although they stood in peril of their lives, Hester felt light as a feather. She felt like shouting from the hilltops that her mother and daddy had not taken the mark.

"Thank you, Lord," she said over again and again in a low whisper.

The captain gave the command for them to be led out to the courtyard. Hester knew the time had come for them to seal their testimony with their own blood. They were led out to a large block three feet high with a swordsman standing by with a shining sword. To the right of the block was a large, deep vat of boiling grease. The three, mother, father, and daughter, were a pathetic scene as they stood close to the block clasping hands. Just how they were to die they did not know, but no matter how cruel, it would soon be over and the victory would be won.

Frank kissed his wife and daughter good-by when he was commanded to come to the block and place his hands on it. Susan was ordered to take her place beside her husband and do likewise. Hester clung to her mother as she took her in her arms and hugged her hungrily to her bosom. The guards shouted at them with oaths, but still they clung to each other until the guards tore them apart.

"Be strong, child," she choked. "Don't recant. We will all meet over on the other side."

Hester was handcuffed to a near by stake, because they thought she would become hysterical. From the place where she stood chained, she could see all that was happening.

Susan and Frank were pale, but calm as they stood there waiting for death. A large number of people who had the mark were gathering to watch them die, and they were giving honor and glory to the Beast. A shrill whistle sounded, and all became silent. The captain, with his eyes glittering and his lips curled into a sneer, drew near the block, and the swordsman stood on the opposite side.

"Frank Wilson, will you renounce your faith in your God and serve the Beast, the true god?"

"No," he said without flinching.

"Then in the name of the Beast, I command that your hands be cut off."

Frank closed his eyes and gritted his teeth together as the swordsman raised his sword and brought it down with great force cutting off both of Frank's hands with one blow and throwing them into the boiling vat of grease. Hester and Susan gave a loud scream of terror. They could hear his hands sizzling and frying as they stood there at the mercy of audacious men.

Susan was asked if she would renounce her faith and take the mark and she answered, "No," with trembling lips; so the swordsman brought the sword down and took both of her hands off, and she gave a shrieking scream of agony. A guard picked them up and threw them into the vat of boiling grease also.

They were asked again if they would recant and take the mark, but the answer was the same, "No," so their ears were cut off and thrown into the boiling grease.

Hester felt as if she were going to faint.

"Oh God, why did we miss the rapture? Why were we so foolish when Your Word told us these times would come? Please, God, help us to be strong. Oh, God," she pleaded, "we need Your help now as we have never needed it before."

After they had refused again to worship the Beast, the guard commanded Frank and Susan to stick their tongues out, and their tongues were cut out.

Hester began to scream hysterically. She wanted to stop screaming, but she did not have the power. A guard shouted for her to shut up, but without success. Another guard ran up and thrust a gag in her mouth, and the only noise she could make then was a gurgling sound. They were possessed with the devil; therefore nothing was too cruel for them to do to a child of God.

The tears rolled down Frank and Susan's cheeks as they went through the beastly tortures. Hester watched as a guard walked up to them with a pointed object and gouged their eyeballs from their sockets. Blood streamed down their faces where their eyeballs had been removed, and blood flowed from the places where different members of their bodies had been cut off by the swordsman. Hester thanked God when she saw her mother had lost consciousness.

They laid her mother on the block and cut her legs off and cast them into the vat of grease. Then her arms were cut off at the shoulders and cast into the sizzling liquid. Finally, her head was cut off and thrown, with the remainder of the body, into the boiling grease.

Hester could see and hear it frying and smell the nauseating odor as it came up to her nostrils. She wanted to close her eyes to shut out the excruciating scene, but a guard stood by keeping an eye on her; and when she closed her eyes, he punched her with the end of his sword.

Twice during the ordeal, she fainted. Each time the ferocious captain ordered the guards to cease the torture of her parents until she was revived, because he wanted her to see it all well done. He was determined to break her spirit. She could not hold out indefinitely. She would have to give in sometime.

Frank was placed on the block. Groans of agony fell from his lips as the hot racking pains shot through his body. His arms, legs and head were cut off and all cast into the boiling vat of grease. Shouts of praise went up in honor of the Beast, but a great calm came over Hester. Her mother and daddy were not suffering any longer.

The gag was removed from her mouth, and her face lighted up with the glory of God.

She shouted in a loud clear voice which startled those standing around, "Thank God, the victory is won! Mother and daddy are safe with the Lord!"

The outburst had come so suddenly and unexpectedly from the frail girl's lips, inspired by the Spirit of God, that many of those with the mark feared and trembled. The hand of a guard was pressed over her mouth so she could say no more, and the handcuffs were removed from her wrist leaving red circles where the steel had cut into her tender flesh.

As she stood there facing the block where her mother and daddy had just died, she felt the victory was almost there for her, too. The captain's piercing eyes rested upon her, but she stood composed. Her heart ceased to beat fast, and the fear of death was gone. Her beautiful dark eyes with their soft light looked searchingly into his cruel ones, and the captain became ill at ease as she continued looking at him unafraid.

"I am ready to die," she said humbly. "Why do you wait?"

That was too much for the audacious captain and it brought a flow of blasphemies from his lips.

"Take her away!" he shouted with a curse. "I am not ready for her to die yet. By the name of the Beast I will break her spirit."

A guard stuck a sword to her back and told her to march toward the prison. Disappointed, she walked in the direction she was told to go. She had wanted to die so very much, but now her desire had been refused. She had nothing to live for but everything to die for. The guard locked her in the same cell where she had been kept before and stomped away.

As soon as his footsteps died away, she drew her Bible from its secret hiding place. With tear-dimmed eyes, she read verse after verse from the Word of God. Why hadn't they killed her? She had not thought for once but what they would. Maybe God had spared her for a purpose and she would understand it all clearly a little later. The thought cheered her heart and made her feel warmer on the inside.

That evening, the guard opened her door and pushed a well-dressed woman of about thirty into the cell with her. She was trembling all over and panting for breath.

"My name is Hester Bell Wilson. Most people call me Hester," she spoke up brightly.

"My—name—is—Silvia—Matthews," the woman stammered in a low voice. "Do they—are they—going—to put you—to death, too? Are you—a Christian?"

"Yes, I am," Hester replied proudly.

The woman moved close to her. She was not afraid of her any longer.

"Maybe you can help me find the Lord. I have tried so hard. You see, my people are prominent people in this city's social world, and they have all taken the mark but me. I guess I would have taken it, too, if it had not been for my nurse Ophelia, who was a wonderful child of God. She told me all about this time and the coming of the Lord. It made a good imaginary story, but I never gave it too much thought other than its just being like any other fairy tale.

"The morning the rapture took place, Ophelia was caught away to be with the Lord, and I realized, for the first time, that the things she had told me all my life were not a made-up story. You see," she continued in a low tone, "my mother and daddy never thought much of church and the Bible.

"My life has never been the same since Ophelia disappeared. I am not interested in the gay crowd I used to run with, and they have all taken the mark. They think I have lost my mind because I refuse to take the mark and I talk about nurse Ophelia and God so much.

"Rather than have me disgrace the family name, they turned me over to the Beast Regime. I heard one of the guards say I would be put to death at sunrise in the morning. It's awful," she choked with tears rushing down her cheeks.

"I know," Hester said with a voice of sympathy. "My mother and daddy were put to death today, and sooner or later I will follow them. I wish it had been today."

The woman stared at Hester with a strange gaze. What kind of girl was this who could be so brave about facing death?

"You mean you are not afraid to die?" she asked in astonishment.

"Well," Hester answered meekly, "the flesh shrinks from the thought of suffering and death, but I felt the Spirit of God in such a marvelous way today. I would have welcomed death so that I could have gone and been with the Lord."

"Then, if you are that close to God," Silvia spoke with great hope in her eyes, "surely you can help me find the Lord. You believe He will save me?" she asked earnestly.

"Yes, honey, by all means I know He will," Hester answered, looking straight into Silvia's eyes.

Hester pulled the Bible from its hiding place and Silvia's eyes lighted up when she saw the Bible, because she knew that was the same Book from which Ophelia had read all those things she told her about. Scripture after scripture was read by Hester while Silvia listened, drinking in each word.

When Hester had finished, she looked up from the pages of God's Holy Writ and asked, "Do you believe what I have been reading to you?"

"Yes," Silvia answered without hesitating, nodding her head.

"Then let us pray that God will save you for Christ's sake."

The two knelt in the musty cell shut in from the eyes of those who hated God's people, and Silvia wept her way through to victory. She arose with her face aglow and amazed at the wonderful strange feeling she had. The thought of dying on tomorrow did not take the joy out of her heart. She had found the Saviour!

The next morning, as the guard stood there ready to take Silvia away, the two new friends clasped hands and promised they would meet on the shore of sweet deliverance.

"Good-by, and thank you for helping me find the Lord," Silvia said, and was led away to her death.

Hester watched with misty eyes from her cell window as Silvia marched bravely to the den of lions. Silvia stood there seemingly without fear, and she shook her head quickly when asked if she would recant before being fed to the hungry lions. Her face lighted up with the glory of God as she raised her hand toward heaven and gave a glorious praise to the living God and walked in a delirium of bliss into the den of lions. The angels in heaven on the street of gold hushed their singing and gave praise to God, because another soul had defeated the Beast and made it through.

Hester's heart was sad, yet it rejoiced at the glorious death of Silvia, because she died in the faith. If it had not been for Hester, she would not have had such a glorious death. Now, she knew why they had not killed her with her parents.

CHAPTER XI

Jim heard a noise like thunder. It was so loud it made the earth rock. Fear clutched his heart as he stood in the open looking up at the sky. What did it mean? He had never heard a noise like that.

If Jim could have looked behind the cloud hanging overhead, he would have seen a shining angel with a trumpet pressed to his lips. Jim waited tensely. What was going to happen?

"Haven't we suffered enough?" Jim choked in his fear. He looked up into the heaven and blasphemed the name of God.

Suddenly, hail and fire mingled with blood began to rain from the skies. It was the most fearful thing Jim had ever seen. Jim ran for a large building that was nearby, and other people were running, screaming, and pushing, trying to get out of the way of the calamity that was falling from the heaven.

Jim watched from a window, and he saw all the green grass burned and a third part of the trees destroyed. Some of the people had not made it to a shelter in time, and their dead bodies were lying in the street. What was this all about? Jim frantically questioned his brain for an answer. Then, he remembered his mother's black Book and the eighth chapter of Revelation telling about it.

"No it can't be!" he shouted. "It can't be! I burned that Book and why should its contents keep coming back to me? I despise it with all my strength. Do you hear?" he cried. "I will not listen to it," he said, but Jim could not get the Scripture out of his mind. It still lingered to haunt him.

When the storm was over, there was another terrible blast, and a second angel from heaven sounded a trumpet, and Jim saw a ball of fire which looked like a great mountain fall from the skies into the sea. Immediately, the redness of the sea which had turned into blood became visible. Jim's heart began to pound furiously as he and other men and women raced for the beach to get a closer view of the sea. It was absurd for the sea to turn into blood, but their eyes were not deceived. It was a fact. As far as Jim could see, it was blood. A third part of the creatures in the sea which had life died, and a third part of the ships were destroyed. The people stood there awe-stricken as they looked at a sick sea vomiting its dead upon the beaches. It was the wrath of God being rained down upon sinful humanity, but the people repented not of their deeds. They blasphemed the name of God.

"And the third angel sounded, and there fell a great star from heaven, burning as it were a lamp, and it fell upon the third part of the rivers, and upon the fountains of waters;

"And the name of the star is called Wormwood: and the third part of the waters became wormwood;

and many men died of the waters, because they were made bitter."—*Revelation 8:10, 11.*

For a number of days now, the city of Alabesta had been without water. What a sickening feeling to go for a drink of water and find it blood. Jim's thirst became unbearable and people were dying of thirst. The cry in the city was water, water. They tried to substitute other liquids, but nothing would quench their thirst and take the place of cool water.

Someone cried, "There is water over yonder," and people went into a wild stampede to get to the place where the crier had said water could be found.

Jim's parched lips ached for good, cold water. He was desperate enough to kill as he rushed madly for the water hole. People, lying along the sidewalks too weak to go, pleaded to those hurrying by to bring them some water; but Jim cursed them and kicked those in his path out of his way. He cared nothing for them. The only person he thought about was Jim.

When Jim got to the water hole, it was surrounded by people down on their knees drinking. The only thing that saved Jim's life was that someone else was in front of him. Jim stood behind a man waiting impatiently for him to finish. The man did not stir.

Jim waited a few moments more then he snarled, "Get up from there, you fool! Don't you know some-one else wants water besides you?"

Still the man did not move. Jim gave him a furious kick with his foot and turned the man face upward. He was dead! Then the words came to Jim: "Many men die of the waters, because they were made bitter."

"That Bible!" he blazed with fury. "I burned that rotten Book. Why should those words come to me? I burned it!" he cried, "and it can't do this to me!"

Jim burned the pages of God's Word, but he could not erase its words from his heart. Man speaks and his words die, but God speaks and they live on forever. His words are words of life. There is no death for them.

In a fit of insane rage, Jim rushed from the water hole which was surrounded by bodies of people who had died from drinking the bitter water. The blasphemies poured from his lips in a mad torrent as he cursed God for sending all those plagues upon them. They had not done anything wrong, so why should He torture them? He was just a cruel being that was trying to run the universe, but it would not be long before the true god, the Beast, would conquer Him and cast Him down forever!

There was a startling interruption of Jim's thoughts as another great noise rent the air.

"And the fourth angel sounded, and the third part of the sun was smitten, and the third part of the moon, and the third part of the stars; so as the third part of them was darkened, and the day shone not for a third part of it, and the night likewise."—*Revelation 8:12.*

The fear that settled in the hearts of mankind when they saw the elements affected in such an unusual manner was indescribable. Day and night the people were reminded of the wrath of God that was being poured out upon the earth.

Suddenly, it began to get dark! Jim stared at his watch and looked around in unbelief.

"It can't be getting dark!" he cried. "It is only twelve o'clock noon. My eyes must be playing tricks on me," he muttered as the darkness continued to get thicker and thicker.

Jim heard a terrific blast just before the darkness began to close in, but he did not see an angel fall from heaven with the key to the bottomless pit and open it. When the angel opened the pit, it was as if a large furnace had been opened, and that was where the darkness was coming from.

About the time Jim decided that night had really settled down upon the earth, the smoke began to clear away. Jim saw the most horrible looking sight he had ever seen in his life. It made the blood run cold in his veins and he felt frozen all over. He wanted to scream, but his lips were numb and his tongue thick. For a few moments, he just stood there and shook with fear.

"And there came out of the smoke locusts upon the earth: and unto them was given power, as the scorpions of the earth have power.

"And it was commanded them that they should not hurt the grass of the earth, neither any green thing, neither any tree; but only those men which have not the seal of God in their foreheads.

"And to them it was given that they should not kill them, but that they should be tormented five months: and their torment was as the torment of a scorpion, when he striketh a man.

"And in those days shall men seek death, and shall not find it; and shall desire to die, and death shall flee from them.

"And the shapes of the locusts were like unto horses prepared unto battle; and on their heads were as it were crowns like gold, and their faces were as the faces of men.

"And they had hair as the hair of women, and their teeth were as the teeth of lions.

"And they had breastplates, as it were breastplates of iron; and the sound of their wings was as the sound of chariots of many horses running to battle.

"And they had tails like unto scorpions, and there were stings in their tails: and their power was to hurt men five months."—*Revelation 9:3-10*.

There was a wild stampede, and people ran over each other trying to get out of the path of the ferocious, tormenting animals of judgment. Those who were attacked screamed pitiful cries for help, but no one could help them. The locusts stung those who had the mark, and they could not get away.

Jim was petrified with fear, but finally the power of motion came back to him, and he ran as fast as his legs would carry him down the street, then across to another street and through an alley. His only thought was to get those terrible animals off his trail. Faster and faster he ran, his breath coming in hard gasps as he heard the shouts and screams of the people he had left behind.

After running many more blocks, dodging this way and that so that they would not find him if they were trailing him, he stopped and listened. The cries of the people had almost faded out; so he felt he was far enough away to rest a little. His chest hurt from the hard breathing and excitement. He sat down on the steps of a brick house and blasphemed the name of God for sending those terrible plagues.

As Jim sat there, his sharp ears picked up a faint sound. He listened attentively. It kept getting louder. His pulse quickened with excitement as he waited, fearful of what the noise might be. Suddenly, around a corner about a block away, the locusts came thundering with mighty speed. The sight of them almost frightened Jim out of his wits. Man had never witnessed such animals on the face of the earth. Their faces were as faces of men, they had hair as the hair of a woman, their teeth were as the teeth of lions, their wings flapped madly, and the crowns on their heads glittered like gold.

Jim jumped to his feet. He was weak all over with fear, but the thought of being attacked by the pursuing creatures drove him on with great speed. He could hear the roar of them getting closer and closer. Oh, if he could only run faster. On they came. It seemed to Jim he could feel their breath on the back of his neck, and cold sweat popped out on his brow. Turning his head to one side and glancing back, he saw them a few yards back. In a few moments they would have him and there was no way of escape.

Stumbling over a stone, he fell, giving a shrieking scream. The ferocious animals were upon him like a lion on its prey. Jim closed his eyes to shut out the horrible sight of them. Frantically, he prayed for the Beast to come to his rescue, but there was no answer to his cry for help. The locusts began to sting him with the dreadful stings in their tails and the fiery pains shot through his body as he was stung again and again. He felt he was afire on the inside of his body. Never had he felt such pains in all his life. He never knew that anything could be so painful as that. Blackness was closing in on him and he felt he was dying, but he did not care. It would be a relief to die and get away from those hideous animals. The last thing Jim remembered was scratching and clawing at the locusts with all his might and blaspheming the name of God.

Hours later he came to, surprised to find himself still alive after the awful ordeal he had gone through. Hot, racking pains shot through his body with untold agony. He was sore and stiff all over, and he cried out with great pain when he tried to move his body. For awhile he lay there too sick to sit up. What torture!

The days passed by with intense suffering. About the time those who carried the mark recovered from an attack of stings by the locusts, they would be attacked again and the suffering was all to go through with again. Jim suffered almost night and day for about five months. When he thought he was getting well from the stings of the dreadful locusts, they would pounce on him again.

People sought to take their own lives but could not, because they were in the five months of the Tribulation Period of which the Bible said: "And in those days shall men seek death, and shall not find it; and shall desire to die, and death shall flee from them."— *Revelation 9:6.*

Some climbed to the top of tall buildings and tried to jump off to end their lives; but when they reached the top, they found they did not have power to jump. Many and various ways, the tortured tried to find death (with guns, swords, knives, and other destructive weapons), but death would flee from them.

"What is the use to live and be tortured all the time? I will end it all," Jim shouted with an oath.

He felt the revolver in his pocket, but he decided it would be easier just to go to the river's bridge and cast himself in. He had always heard it said that drowning was an easy death; so he started for the river's bridge. How the hatred boiled in his heart for the so-called God who had sent all those plagues upon them, but one day, he thought, He would be defeated by the Beast.

After a long eternity, he came to the bridge. Looking down into the cool water, he thought it would not be long until it would all be over. He stood at the edge and tried to jump down into the water, but to his amazement, he was not able. He tried again and again, but each time was without success. Then the words came to him: "And in those days shall men seek death, and shall not find it; and shall desire to die, and death shall flee from them."—*Revelation 9:6*.

Jim whirled around in a rage. "Who said that?" he blazed. "Who said I can't die!"

Suddenly, it dawned upon him where those words came from.

"That damnable Book called the Bible! I wish it would leave me alone! What is it to tell a person what they can and cannot do? Down through the ages man has taken his life if he wanted to," he said scornfully.

With his hand raised toward heaven, he swore with an oath that he would take his life. Jerking his small revolver from his pocket, he put it to the side of his head and tried to pull the trigger, but try as hard as he could, to his astonishment, he did not have power to pull the trigger. He fell down on the bridge blaspheming the name of God.

From the same direction that Jim had come to the bridge, there appeared a frail figure hurrying to get across the bridge. The girl was haggard and very scared. It was Mary Conway, the girl who attended the same church that Hester and Mother Collins had attended.

Mary had been through many things, but she had not taken the mark. She would have never dared cross the bridge in daylight if it had not been that her life was in great danger. Some men of the Beast Regime had almost caught her, so she had to take a chance crossing the bridge and try to escape. It was her only hope. Gasping for breath, she hurried along casting a furtive glance behind every few yards.

She felt she would welcome death if she were a Christian, but she had not been able to find the Lord. If she could only believe, but it was so hard to believe. The earth had been turned over into the hands of the devil, and when she tried to pray, she seemed as one being mocked.

When she got to the edge of the bridge, she stopped, looked all around; then almost holding her breath, she entered the bridge. In her fright of the men pursuing her, she did not notice the figure of Jim lying on the bridge until she was almost upon him.

Hearing her footsteps Jim cried, "Help! Help!"

Mary started to rush on, but then she thought it might be a child of God, and he could help her find the Lord; so against her better judgment, she went to the pathetic figure.

At first, Mary did not recognize Jim. His hair was long and uncombed; he had not shaven in days and his clothes were dirty and torn. Her heart beat faster. There was something strangly familiar about him. It was as if she had known him, yet he was drastically different from the person she had known. He moved his head with agony to one side so he could see her better; then she recognized him.

"Jim!" she cried, falling down on her hands and knees, forgetting about the danger of her own life, and lifting his head from the hard bridge with her rough hands which had once been soft and pretty.

"Jim, don't you know me?" she asked with great joy. There were tears of gladness in her eyes, because she had found Jim.

"Jim, this is Mary," she went on in a spasmodic tone.

Jim had known Mary all her life. They had gone to school together. Mary did not have a brother, so Jim had been her big brother, and she idolized him. Jim was older than Mary, and while she was still in the lower grades, he finished school and went away to college.

"Jim!" she cried, "you missed the rapture! Your mother was under such a burden for you that last night before—before she went away," she choked, with two big tears rolling down her cheeks. "I thought sure you had gotten saved and had made the rapture. Jim, have you found the Lord?" she asked anxiously, holding her ear a little closer.

"What do you mean found the Lord?" Jim snarled with bitterness. "You see that gun over there? Pick it up and take my life."

"Oh, no! Jim!" she exclaimed. "I could not do a thing like that. Let's try to pray. God can help us."

With this, Jim went into a rage.

"Away with God!" he shouted, raising his right hand.

Mary stared in overwhelming wonder. Jim had the Mark of the Beast! She seemed to be smothering on the inside. Cold sweat was on her brow as she finally managed to get to her feet. Her friend she had regarded with fervent devotion and affection so many years was now her enemy.

Jim glared at her as she stood to her feet and began to back away and said, "You see that gun over there? Pick it up and take my life! It is your only way out, because if you don't, I will sound this whistle, and you know what that will mean for you."

"No, Jim!" she cried hysterically. "I can't! I can't!"

Turning away from him, she ran for the other side of the bridge.

"Come back!" Jim shouted, "Come back! you fool!"

A shrill whistle which sent cold chills through Mary's body pierced the air. She knew the Beast Regime would be after her at once. Before she reached the end of the bridge, she heard footsteps running behind her and men's voices shouting, "Stop! Stop!"

On she ran praying, "Oh God, don't let them take me. Don't let them take me. I am not saved."

She made a desperate attempt to run faster, but her weary legs, weak from fear and hunger, would not speed up. The men were getting closer and closer; then rough hands reached out and grabbed her, and she found herself staring into the eyes of devil-possessed men. They gave honor and glory to the Beast as they almost dragged her along.

"Please God," she prayed, fear enveloping her heart and about to smother the life from her body, "don't let them kill me before I find You."

They led her through the gate to the courtyard of torture, and instead of taking her to the prison, they took her straight to the block to take her life.

"Please don't kill me!" she cried. "I am not saved! Please let me have a little while to pray," but they paid her no attention.

The guard stepped forward with a shining sword in his hand. She stood there, bewildered and helpless, and it seemed God-forsaken.

"Oh God, save my soul," she cried, but all was dark, and she could not contact God.

She was asked the question, "Will you take the mark?"

She was trembling all over. How sad to die without hope and without God. Mary was aware of the fact if she gave her life it would not save her. She must have a "born-again" experience through the blood of the Son of God.

Determined not to take the mark, she shook her head and said, "No! I won't take the mark, but please, please don't kill me."

Merciless hands laid her on the block, and the swordsman drew back the glittering sword to take her head from her shoulders, but there was a startling

interruption as a soldier rushed up to the swordsman
and gave the salute of the Beast Regime:

"The Beast live forever!"

The swordsman dropped the sword as if it were a
hot iron and gave the salute: "The Beast live forever!"

"The Beast has come to the city and will pass this
way in a few minutes," he said with excitable ges-
tures. "Open the gates for he wants to pass through
the torturing ground."

They did not wait for more. Many rushed out of
the gate and down the street in the direction the messenger had come. Mary was lifted from the block
with extreme cruelty and rushed to a prison cell.
What a relief it was to know that she would be spared
a little longer. Maybe she could find the Lord.

She crept to the tiny barred window and timidly
looked out. From her window, she could look through
the open gate down the street. The sight she saw
almost took her breath. Thousands of people lined
the street as far as her eyes could see. Many of them
were down on their knees with their faces buried
in the ground. The shouts of long live the Beast,
hallelujahs, honors, and glories went up to the Beast
with blood curdling horror to those who did not have
the mark.

Just then, a chariot appeared drawn by six gor-
geous white horses. It was breath taking in its beauty.
The chariot was overlaid with all manner of precious
stones—sapphire, jasper, emerald, chalcedony, ame-

thyst, chrysoprasus, and jacinth. The wheels sparkled with diamonds as they slowly turned around and around. The horses' gears were gold studded with diamonds. It was the most beautiful thing Mary had ever seen.

The man who rode in the chariot was horrifying. He had a fierce countenance with eyes as flames of fire. He wore a white robe dotted with large sparkling diamonds and a gold sash was tied around his waist. The tassel of his exclusive turban swayed and glittered with tiny precious stones.

Suddenly, the procession stopped. The Antichrist sat in his chariot and the Antispirit, with a garment similar to the Beast, stood in front of him and looked into the heaven and commanded fire to come down. Immediately, the heaven lighted up and fire fell before the eyes of the people. Some without the mark, watching from the shadows of buildings, came rushing out and fell down on their faces declaring that the Beast was God when they saw the miracle.

Mary felt a great spirit of worship come over her as she watched from her cell window. There was a superb power trying to force her to her knees, but she knew it was not the true God. She must not be deceived and bow down to him.

The procession started moving again, and the people shouted with a voice which sounded like the voice of many waters, "The Beast is the true God! The Beast live forever!"

The chariot passed through the gate, and then it was even with the prison. The Beast was looking straight ahead, but then his penetrating eyes suddenly focused on Mary and burned her flesh. She never thought anyone could have so much power over her. She felt as if she must bow down and worship.

"Please God, I plead the blood. I plead the blood of Jesus," she choked.

Her face was turning the color of paste as the Beast's piercing eyes seemed to look right into her very soul and read every thought of her heart. Mary was weak all over, but she clung to the bars of the window to keep from bowing down. There was a look of triumph on the Beast's face as he saw the agony he was putting her through. If he had stared at her one minute longer, she would have fallen down and worshiped him, his power was so great over her. His eyes turned from her, as the chariot slowly moved on up the street. She sank to the floor, and her body shook with uncontrollable sobs.

"Oh God," she cried with a deplorable feeling, "please help me to believe."

As Mary lay on the hard floor of the cell, she heard a noise like thunder. She listened. The shrieks and screams of many people out in the street went up. What could it be that had brought such a sudden change over them? There were no more praises going up in honor of the Beast. Her pulse quickened.

She got to the window just in time to see the chariot of the Beast in all its glory being lifted by unseen power into the air. The six horses, chariot, Antichrist, and Antispirit arose like a great bird and disappeared in the clouds. Mary stood appalled at the sight she witnessed. It was like magic.

The screams of terror from the people caused her shrewd eyes to look anxiously down the street in search for the cause of the distress. Suddenly, her eyes went wide in horror, for coming down the street were many hundreds of lions with men riding on their backs. No, they were not exactly lions. They had heads like lions, but they had bodies like horses, tails like serpents with heads, and they were biting the people. The riders on the odd looking animals had breastplates of fire, jacinth, and brimstone, and out of the mouths of the horses boiled fire, smoke, and brimstone. They were devouring many of the people who got in their path. It was maddening to watch them. They were the lion headed horses that John told about in the ninth chapter of Revelation:

"And the number of the army of the horsemen were two hundred thousand thousand: and I heard the number of them.

"And thus I saw the horses in the vision, and them that sat on them, having breastplates of fire, and of jacinth, and brimstone: and the heads of the horses were as the heads of lions; and out of their mouths issued fire and smoke and brimstone.

"For their power is in their mouth, and in their tails: for their tails were like unto serpents, and had heads, and with them they do hurt."—*Revelation 9:16, 17, 19.*

It was like a nightmare to Mary as she stared with bewilderment at the horses of destruction and their riders. People ran for weapons to protect themselves and many shots were fired, but it did not have any power on the riders. They rode straight through the city leaving many dead in their path. The roar of them sounded like thunder in the distance as they galloped on through the city leaving the street covered with dead, wounded, dying, and bleeding people. It looked like a great battlefield. The people who were left alive did not honor the God of heaven or repent of their wicked deeds, but they blasphemed His Holy Name, and God rained more plagues from heaven.

The first angel in the sixteenth chapter of Revelation poured out his vial upon the earth, and a grievous sore broke out on those who had the Mark of the Beast or had worshiped his image. Jim broke out all over with the horrible sores. What pain and agony they caused, and he could find no relief from them.

When a second angel poured out his vial upon the sea, it became as the blood of a dead man, and every living thing in the sea died.

The third angel poured out his vial upon the rivers and fountains of waters and they became blood, and the angel of the waters said:

"Thou art righteous, O Lord, which art, and wast, and shalt be, because thou hast judged thus. For they have shed the blood of saints and prophets, and thou hast given them blood to drink; for they are worthy."

Another out of the altar said, "Even so, Lord God Almighty, true and righteous are Thy judgments."

The sun began to get brighter and brighter. People sought refuge from the sun, but there was no place they could find that would not be affected by its heat. The sun got so hot that it scorched men with its heat; but they did not repent, for they hated God and his judgments.

After the sun got so unbearably hot, it suddenly began to get dimmer and dimmer until it refused to shine at all, because an angel had poured out a vial upon the seat of the Beast, and darkness began to settle down. The darkness got thicker and thicker. It got so dark that Jim, along with all the others who had the mark, gnawed his tongue for pain.

CHAPTER XII

That day when Mary was brought in by the Beast Regime, Hester was standing at her cell window. She saw the guards bringing someone into the courtyard, and as they drew closer with their prisoner, her heart missed a beat. It was Mary Conway, the girl from Fairview church whom Hester had always admired. She heard Mary cry for mercy and for them not to kill her.

"My God," Hester prayed, "don't let them put Mary to death before she finds You. Please God, make the way for me to talk to her and help her get saved."

Through her tears, she saw the guard lay Mary on the block. She was frantic with anxiety as she watched, and it looked as if the Lord were not going to answer her prayer. All hope of Mary's being rescued from death vanished.

Hester closed her eyes and her lips moved in prayer when she saw the swordsman draw back his sword to take Mary's head from her shoulders. When she opened her eyes again, she was shocked to see the swordsman had dropped the sword by his side and was talking to someone; then she saw Mary being taken up from the death block and being taken toward the prison.

In a few minutes, she heard footsteps coming down the hall. She listened, holding her breath. That was probably Mary, and she was anxious to know where they put her. They stopped just before they got to her cell, and she heard the key rattle in the lock of the cell next to hers.

"Oh God," she prayed, "let it be Mary that is being locked in that cell so I can talk to her." With eyes glistening with tears, she fell down on her knees, humbly thanking the Lord for sparing Mary.

She watched from her cell window and saw the procession of the Beast pass through the gates of the prison.

Later, after most of the excitement had quieted around the prison, she went to the wall, which separated her cell and the one they had just put someone in before the Beast came through, and called, "Mary," in a low whisper. Her heart beat faster as she listened, but no one answered.

Then she called again, a little louder.

Her heart leaped with joy when she heard Mary's voice on the other side of the wall saying, "Who is it? Who is calling my name?"

In her great joy, Hester forgot all about the guards. "It's Hester," she cried with a joyful voice, "Hester Bell Wilson. Don't you remember the girl with black hair that used to go to the same church that you and Mother Collins went to?"

Mary's heart was jumping so with excitement, it felt as if it were going to jump out of her bosom.

"Oh, Hester, are you saved?" she asked with great anxiety.

She held her breath until the joyful answer came back.

"Yes, Mary. Thank God I have found Him."

"Hester I am so glad you have found the Lord. I have sought Him so hard, but it is so difficult for me to believe. I wish I could believe. I would if I could, but I can't."

"Listen, Mary," Hester spoke breathlessly, "do you have a Bible?"

"Yes, I have a New Testament."

"Well, that is all right. I have a Bible, too. Wait a minute until I get it."

Like a flash she was back at the stone wall with the Bible.

"Now, Mary, turn with me to the passages of Scripture that I tell you and read them."

Mary did as she was told. Verse after verse she read, then one girl knelt on one side of the wall, and the other girl knelt on the other side, and they prayed for Mary's salvation; but Mary could not believe.

The days passed by and Hester continued praying with Mary and reading the Word of God with her. Sometimes Mary felt it was no use to pray as she sank deeper into the dungeon of despair and doubt. She was surrounded by the demon powers of darkness, and her cell seemed to be infested with them.

One morning, the key rattled in the lock of Hester's door and a guard stood there saying with a voice of doom, "Hester Bell Wilson, your final chance has come. You will either take the mark this day or we are prepared to take your life. You will be burned as a heretic at the stake."

For a moment Hester was startled. Although she had been expecting this time to come, it was shocking when it did come, but she soon gained her composure.

"Wait just one moment. I have something I want to take with me, because I will not be coming back any more."

She reached under the dirty mattress of her cot and pulled out her black Book. The guard stared at it incredulously. It could not be possible that she had kept a book like that concealed in her cell. He was seized with a fit of anger as he stood watching the girl hugging her Bible to her bosom.

"You know what we do with Books like that?" he asked sternly.

Hester nodded her head sadly. She had seen the guards of the Beast Regime pile Bibles in stacks, pour gas on them and set them on fire and blaspheme God's name while they burned. Sometimes they stacked them around the heretic and burned them as they burned a child of God.

"Give me that Book!" he said furiously, snatching at the Bible.

As his hand touched the Book he let out an oath and drew it back quickly. It was as if he had taken hold of a hot iron.

"What have you done to that cursed Book?" he snarled angrily.

"I haven't done anything," Hester said in surprise. "It is just as it has always been."

"Well, come on and carry it yourself," he said harshly.

Mary heard every word from her cell. Hester was going to be put to death! Now there would be no one to help her find the Lord. Hester had been such a blessing to her. It would be her time to die soon, too, and she did not know the Lord.

"Mary," Hester called just as the guard led her out of the cell, "the victory has come. It is time for me to go home. Mary, honey, believe the Lord as I told you, and He will save you. This is farewell," she said with a sob, "until we meet around the throne of God. I will pray for you until the last," she added meekly.

"Oh, no! Hester!" Mary screamed hysterically, "they can't put you to death! They can't!" she cried.

"Good-by, Hester," she said with tears rolling down her cheeks as Hester was marched on up the hall. "Good-by," and then in a low quivering murmur she added, "until we meet around the throne of God."

Why had she said that? She had no hope. She could not believe.

Mary crept over to the window and looked out. A crowd had gathered to watch Hester die. She walked between two guards with her face lighted up with the glory of God. In her hand was clutched her precious Book. Several guards reached for the Book, but they had the same experience as the one who took her from the cell. The ferocious captain reached for it after he saw a number of guards jerk their hands back, and it burned his hand also.

With an oath he commanded, "Burn that damnable Book with her. She has bewitched it."

She walked straight as a soldier with her head and shoulders held erect. A great calm had come over her, and she was not afraid any longer. Her lips moved in prayer as she was chained to the stake, and Mary, watching from her cell window with tear dimmed eyes, knew that Hester was praying for her.

The guards piled the wood around her, and then she was asked if she would recant and take the mark. A graveyard quietness settled down over the crowd as they watched and waited breathlessly for the decision of the beautiful girl. Her eyes sparkled like diamonds, and there was a halo of glory about her head. She did not hesitate to give her answer.

In a sweet voice which sounded like heavenly music she said, "No. Ten thousand times no. Soon I will be with Him who died for me. Thank God for His wonderful Son, Jesus, who bled and died on Calvary that I might live."

For a moment the crowd was awe-stricken, then as one person, their voices were lifted in blasphemies to the God which Hester had given honor and glory; then the command was given.

Mary stood at the window with her breath coming in hard, short gasps, and her finger nails dug into her flesh as she clenched her fists.

The fire was kindled, and the yellow flames began to lick hungrily for Hester's body. She stood there chained to the stake and her Bible held to her heart with both hands. Her lips still moved in prayer as she looked into the heaven. The flames mounted higher and higher until she was surrounded by the red, hot flames, but she did not seem to feel the pain.

Her voice rang out with the power of God just before she died.

" 'Tis so sweet to trust Him;" then one last shout, "Thank God the victory has come."

How could she be so bold and happy even in death?—Mary wondered.

Suddenly, through the flames, she saw two shining angels whose garments were brighter than the flames of fire. They stood on each side of Hester and braced her. God had sent His ministering spirits to strengthen her and help her die the victorious death.

Mary fell down on her face on the cell floor and her body shook with sobs.

"My God," she cried bitterly, "why didn't I make the rapture? I heard about it all my life. I have been such a fool."

As she lay there sobbing, the iron door opened and a guard shouted at her with an oath, "Get up from there and stop acting like a fool! I have come for you. It is time for you to die!"

Mary froze. They were going to put her to death and she had not found the Lord. She looked wildly around her cold cell with the pile of straw in the corner which had been her bed. It was so terrible to die without God.

"Please," she said in a meek pleading voice, "give me just a little longer."

"You have had plenty of time to make your decision," he answered. "Come!" he said, roughly taking hold of her arm and jerking her toward the door.

She walked down the hall with trembling limbs, her little Testament held tightly in her hand and praying frantically, "Oh God, please help. Please help. I am about to be put to death. Oh—God—," she choked, "I just can't die without You."

Although she cried again and again, there did not seem to be a God to hear. Mary's face was pale and drawn, her eyes were haggard, and she was very gaunt. She saw the death block ahead of her, and the swordsman standing with the sword in his hand waiting to take her life. Her knees felt so weak, she did not know if she could make it the rest of the way or not. Her eyes met Jim's and he gave a hideous laugh which made her weaker.

Finally, she stood before the block.

"God, please help me!" she prayed, "Help me, God!" she cried, but there was no answer.

Mary was asked by the audacious captain, "Will you take the mark?"

Her heart pounded like mad. The time that she had dreaded so long had come, and although God had not saved her, she would not take the mark.

"No," she cried, shaking like a leaf and staring into space. "I cannot take the mark. He has not saved me, and it seems that I cannot touch Him, but I know that Jesus died for me."

For the first time, there was a glimmer of real faith. She repeated it again as one in a daze. The veil of doubt and darkness was moved aside by the Holy Spirit of God. She saw Calvary in all its shame and suffering; Calvary in all its power and glory. She saw the Son of God hanging on Calvary with the blood running from his pierced hands. She saw Him look at her and His lips moved and He said to her: "Child, I died for you. My blood still has power to wash away your sins if you will only believe."

Her countenance lighted up with the glory of God, and her eyes began to shine like two, big stars as she shouted triumphantly, "I do believe! I do believe! I have found Him! I have found the Christ of God!"

Then she began to sing:

> *"What can wash away my sin?*
> *Nothing but the blood of Jesus;*
> *What can make me whole again?*
> *Nothing but the blood of Jesus."*

In her bliss of glory, she lost sight of those who had gathered to watch her die. The guards shouted for her to hush, but as one in a trance she sang on. Great fear seized those that stood by.

"Put her to death! Quick! She has gone insane!" the captain shouted with trembling lips.

They laid her down on the block, but she did not feel their rough hands at all. She sang on. The singing was so beautiful that even the angels in heaven laid aside their harps and hushed their singing to listen. The swordsman drew back his sword bringing it down with mighty force, but Mary did not feel the pain. On the shore of sweet deliverance she lifted her eyes, and an angel put a shining white robe on her. She picked up a palm and stood before the throne praising her God and shouting, "Holy, holy, Lord God Almighty."

Mary was one in that great multitude that John saw in the seventh chapter of Revelation.

"I beheld, and, lo, a great multitude, which no man could number, of all nations, and kindreds, and people, and tongues, stood before the throne, and before the Lamb, clothed with white robes, and palms in their hands;

"And cried with a loud voice, saying, Salvation to our God which sitteth upon the throne, and unto the Lamb.

"And all the angels stood round about the throne, and about the elders and the four beasts, and fell before the throne on their faces, and worshiped God.

"Saying, Amen: Blessing, and glory, and wisdom, and thanksgiving, and honour, and power, and might, be unto our God for ever and ever. Amen.

"And one of the elders answered, saying unto me, What are these which are arrayed in white robes? and whence came they?

"And I said unto him, Sir, thou knowest. And he said to me, These are they which came out of great tribulation, and have washed their robes, and made them white in the blood of the Lamb.

"Therefore are they before the throne of God, and serve Him day and night in His temple: and he that sitteth on the throne shall dwell among them.

"They shall hunger no more, neither thirst any more; neither shall the sun light on them, nor any heat.

"For the Lamb which is in the midst of the throne shall feed them, and shall lead them unto living fountains of waters: and God shall wipe away all tears from their eyes."

Jim stood and watched Mary die. He detested the sight of her, and he was glad that she was being put to death. Her head rolled down into the gutter; and Jim picked it up by the hair, and like a maniac, he slung it around and around, shouting honor and glory to the Beast.

Just as Jim put the bodiless head down, an excited messenger rushed up and told him that in a certain province they were having a terrible hailstorm, and the hailstones were falling out of the skies weighing almost a hundred pounds. They were destroying everything in their path.

Suddenly, the old earth began to shake with mighty force. The sun became black as sackcloth of hair, and the moon became as blood. The stars of heaven fell unto the earth, even as a fig tree casteth her untimely figs when she is shaken of a mighty wind. The heaven departed as a scroll when it is rolled together; and every mountain and island was moved out of its place.

As the stars fell from heaven, the sun refused to shine, the moon turned into blood, the mountains and islands moved, people were more frightened than they had been at any time since God had started raining judgment down upon sinful humanity.

Jim and all the people looked up into the heaven with great fear and saw the heaven open and the Son of God appear on a white horse. His eyes were as a flame of fire, and on His head were many crowns. He had a name written that no man knew but Him Himself. He was clothed with a vesture dipped in blood, and His name is called The Word of God. The armies which were in heaven followed Him upon white horses. They were clothed in fine linen, white and clean.

As Jim looked in horror, he saw a two edged sword go out of His mouth with great fierceness. On His vesture and on His thigh a name was written: KING OF KINGS, AND LORD OF LORDS. He was coming as a roaring lion to rain vengeance upon those on the earth who had the mark.

Those who had the mark went into a wild frenzy and ran for the rocks and the mountains. All Jim's boldness was gone now, and he fell down below the huge rocks and mountains and pleaded for them to fall on him.

"Fall on me!" he cried frantically "I can't ever face Him! Rocks be merciful!" he prayed. "Fall on me and bury me so deep beneath your gigantic weight that I will never have to face Him! I have taken the mark! I have sold my soul to the devil and there is no forgiveness for me! I am denied heaven," he groaned. "He died for me, but I did not appreciate His sacrifice. I trampled His blood under foot as if it was something unholy," he choked. "There is no mercy for me. I rejected the nail-riven hand that was pierced for me.

"I shall stand at the white throne of judgment, and the judge of all the earth shall say, 'Depart from me you cursed into the everlasting fire prepared for the devil and his angels which burneth with fire and brimstone forever and ever."

"Fall on me! Fall on me rocks and mountains!" he shrieked with heart-rending screams. "The day of His wrath has come! I would repent, but there is no repentance for me. I am lost! I am eternally lost!" he wailed with a shriek which sounded like one from the bottomless pit of hell.

THE END.

From the jungles of Ecuador to a tiny watchshop in Holland to behind the Iron Curtain—thrill to the very real human drama of ordinary people who suddenly find themselves empowered by God's love to do *extraordinary* things . . .